THE OLIVET DISCOURSE MADE *EASY*

THE OLIVET DISCOURSE MADE *EASY*

A Made *Easy* Series™ Book

Kenneth L. Gentry, Jr., Th.D.

Chesnee, South Carolina 29323
"Proclaiming the kingdom of God and teaching those things which concern the Lord Jesus Christ, with all confidence."
(Acts 28:31)

Kenneth L. Gentry, Jr., Th. M.,Th. D.
(c) Copyright 2010 by Gentry Family Trust udt April 2, 1999
    Reprint 2021 with slight corrections

The Made *Easy* Series™ provides substantial studies on significant issues in a succinct and accessible format from an evangelical and Reformed perspective.

Published by:
Victorious Hope Publishing
P.O. Box 285
Chesnee, South Carolina 29323

www.VictoriousHope.com

Printed in the United States of America

978-1-7343620-4-6

All rights reserved. No part of this book may be reproduced in any form or by any means, except for brief quotations for the purpose of review, comment, or scholarship, without written permission from the publisher.

Victorious Hope Publishing is committed to producing Christian educational materials for promoting the whole Bible for the whole of life. We are conservative, evangelical, and Reformed and are committed to the doctrinal formulation found in the Westminster Standards.

Dedicated to

Rev. T. J. Gentry, Th.D.

Friend and Encourager
(I even like his last name)

TABLE OF CONTENTS

Abbreviations... ix
Preface xi
1. Olivet's Narrative Context (Matthew 1–22) 1
2. Olivet's Specific Impetus (Matthew 23) 27
3. Olivet's Central Focus (Matthew 24:1–3) 39
4. Olivet's Interpretive Key (Matthew 24:34) 51
5. False Expectations of the End (Matthew 24:4–14) 65
6. The Beginning of the End (Matthew 24:15–28) 87
7. The Coming of the End (Matthew 24:29–31) 107
8. The Transition Passage (Matthew 24:32–36) 127
9. Conclusion... 139

Select Scripture Index 143
Subject and Name Index 151

ABBREVIATIONS

Abot R. Nat.	*The Fathers According to Rabbi Nathan*
Ann	*The Annals of Rome* by Cornelius Tacitus
Ant.	*Jewish Antiquities* by Flavius Josephus
Apion	*Against Apion* by Flavius Josephus
b.	*The Babylonian Talmud*
BAGD	*A Greek-English Lexicon of the New Testament and Other Early Christian Literature.* 3d. ed. Rev. by Frederick William Danker. Chicago: University of Chicago Press, 2000.
BKC	*Bible Knowledge Commentary*
EBC	*The Expositor's Bible Commentary*
Eccl Hist	Eusebius, *Ecclesiastical History*
Embassy	*Embassy to Gaius* by Philo Judaeus
ESV	English Standard Version
Hist	*The Histories* by Cornelius Tacitus
ICC	International Critical Commentary
Legate	*Legatio ad Gaiuim (On the Embassy to Gaius)* by Philo
J.W.	*The Jewish War* by Flavius Josephus
Life	*The Life of Flavius Josephus* by Flavius Josephus
m.	*The Mishnah*
MBC	Moody Bible Commentary
NASB	New American Standard Bible
Nat Hist	*Natural History* by Pliny the Elder
NICNT	New International Commentary on the New Testament
NIGTC	New International Greek Testament Commentary
N.B.	New Jerusalem Bible
NKJV	New King James Version
NTC	New Testament Commentary
PEBP	*The Popular Encyclopedia of Bible Prophecy*. Ed. by Tim LaHaye and Ed Hinson. Eugene, Ore.: Harvest House, 2004.
Spec. Laws	*On the Special Laws* by Philo Judaeus

Special Note

In order to facilitate research by scholar and layman alike, references to Josephus' works will combine the older, more generally known Whiston numbering system of 1737 with the current Loeb Classical Library system. Thus, Whiston's numbering of *J.W.* 6:1:8 would appear with both his numbering and Loeb's as *J.W.* 6:1:8 [81–92]). Or when directly quoting a scholar who uses Loeb's, I will include the Whiston numbering system in brackets. For instance, if I cite a paragraph from a scholar who refers to *J.W.* 2:125, it will appear as: *J.W.* 2:125 [2:8:4]. I will however be employing Whiston's translation rather than Loeb's in that it is more easily (and inexpensively!) accessible to a general audience — for whom this "Made *Easy* Series" is written.

PREFACE

Few texts of Scripture are more fascinating than our Lord's prophecy known as the Olivet Discourse. As a young, newly-converted, sixteen-year-old Christian I remember being mesmerized with this glorious passage of Scripture. It seemed so clear that we were living in the days that would finally give way to the "great tribulation."

My pastor (Rev. John S. Lanham, my uncle) taught eloquently and often on the Olivet Discourse from a dispensationlist perspective. He let me work at his Christian bookstore (Lanham's Bible Bookshop) where I was able to purchase many Christian books at discount on this my favorite topic. I had a voracious appetite for biblical prophecy, and especially for the Olivet Discourse. One of my favorite books was Hal Lindsey's newly-published *Late Great Planet Earth*.

In my early-twenties I also enjoyed studying prophecy under Kay Arthur at Reachout Youth Ranch in Chattanooga, Tennessee. (Kay is well-known now for her Precepts Ministries.) I well remember going to the Tivoli Theater in downtown Chattanooga to watch her perform a one-woman play she had written which was a dramatic enactment of the great tribulation.

I had such a zeal for studying Scripture — and especially biblical prophecy — that I eventually left the engineering program at the University of Tennessee, Chattanooga, and enrolled in a dispensationalist college, Tennessee Temple College. There I was able to study Bible at an academic level in a systematic fashion. One of my favorite courses at TTC was an upper- level course taught by Dr. Dennis Wisdom: course number BI-317, "Premillennialism." Dr. Wisdom ably presented the case for dispensationalism to a class full of stalwart ministerial students hoping to graduate before the rapture.

Upon graduating college in 1973 with a B.A. degree in Biblical Studies (and a minor in Greek), I moved to Winona Lake, Indiana, to continue my studies. There I enrolled at Grace Theological Seminary, a Grace Brethren school deeply-committed to dispensationalism. Now my studies were moving to an even deeper level in this graduate program.

While at Grace Seminary I began to question some of the doctrine I was being taught. In one class I was researching Acts 2 and noticed that

Peter was preaching the resurrection of Christ in a way that suggested he saw it as the Lord's enthronement:

> Brethren, I may confidently say to you regarding the patriarch David that he both died and was buried, and his tomb is with us to this day. And so, because he was a prophet, and knew that God had sworn to him with an oath to seat one of his descendants upon his throne, he looked ahead and spoke of the resurrection of the Christ (Acts 2:29–31).

This shook my dispensationalism to its very foundation. This indicated that Christ is enthroned *now*; he is not awaiting the rapture and the great tribulation before assuming his kingship.

As a consequence of this insight I began reading eschatological works from other evangelical perspectives. In this wider reading I stumbled upon an older work (1945) by O. T. Allis: *Prophecy and the Church*. This book so thoroughly dismantled dispensationalism as a viable eschatological system that I left it for good. After researching available schools, I decided to transfer to Reformed Theological Seminary in Jackson, Mississippi.

At Reformed Seminary I took a course that became a life-changing experience for me: "History and Eschatology." In this course the instructor, Greg L. Bahnsen, taught from a preterist perspective — a position I knew absolutely nothing about, despite its prominence as a widely-spread evangelical option in the 1800s. In the class Bahnsen directed us to two studies on the Olivet Discourse: J. Marcellus Kik's *The Eschatology of Victory* and Jay E. Adams' *The Time Is at Hand*.

I was absolutely bowled over by both of these works. Despite having frequently read and studied Matthew 24, I had never really noticed that it clearly states that "this generation will not pass away until all these things take place" (Matt 24:34). How could this be? Was not the great tribulation in *our* future? Why did Christ make it sound to his disciples as if it were in *their* near future?

After carefully studying the issues I became firmly convinced of preterism. Preterism is the belief that many (not all) of the judgment prophecies of the New Testament were fulfilled in the first century at the destruction of the temple in AD 70. Now I understood the catastrophic consequences of the transition from the old covenant, temple-based economy to the New Testament, spiritual economy. God removed his temple from the earth so that men might seek him in spiritual, non-bloody worship. As the Lord Jesus taught the Samaritan woman:

> an hour is coming when neither in this mountain, nor in Jerusalem, shall you worship the Father.... An hour is coming, and now is, when the

true worshipers shall worship the Father in spirit and truth; for such people the Father seeks to be His worshipers." (John 4:20, 23)

As the writer to Hebrews put it: "When He said, 'A new covenant,' He has made the first obsolete. But whatever is becoming obsolete and growing old is ready to disappear" (Heb 8:13). At last, I understood more fully what it meant to be a new covenant Christian.

Over the years I have engaged in much preaching, lecturing, and writing on the preterist approach to the Olivet Discourse. As I have studied more deeply, some of my positions within the preterist approach have shifted. But my preterism has been confirmed time-and-time again.

In this brief work I present the interested reader with a careful, exegetically-rigorous analysis of Jesus' teaching in Matthew 24. I hope you will read it with your Bible and you mind open. I think you will find this approach quite compelling

Come, let us reason together!

Kenneth L. Gentry, Th.D.
Director, GoodBirth Ministries

Chapter 1
OLIVET'S NARRATIVE CONTEXT
Matthew 1–22

In Matthew 24 and 25 the Lord presents the last of five major discourses around which Matthew structures his Gospel.[1] Though we find the same material in Mark 13 and Luke 21, Matthew's lengthy version is the best known. Since he presents this material while on the Mount of Olives (Matt 24:3) it is called the Olivet Discourse. Within this long teaching section we come upon that terrifying era known as the great tribulation.

Confusion Regarding Olivet

Christ's teaching on the great tribulation has long intrigued and transfixed Christians. This is especially true in the modern evangelical church today. What Bible-believing Christian has not been alarmed by Christ's prophetic warning about a time in which men will experience "wars and rumors of wars" (Matt 24:6)? "Famines and earthquakes" (Matt 24:7)? "False prophets" who "will mislead many" (Matt 24:10)? The "abomination of desolation" (Matt 24:15)? "False Christs" (Matt 24:24)? Who has not dreaded the time when "the sun will be darkened, and the moon will not give its light" (Matt 24:29)? These are fearsome images presented by our Lord to his people.

Christians today are absolutely fascinated by all of these issues arising during that terrible period known as "the great tribulation" (Matt 24:21). Numerous multimillion, best-selling Christian books have been written on this fateful time in human history. The big sales really began in earnest in 1970 with Hal Lindsey's *The Late Great Planet Earth*. This book was one of the largest-selling books of the last century, generating sales of over thirty-five million copies and translation into fifty-four languages. Tim LaHaye's multi-volume series *Left Behind*, which began publication in

---

[1] Those five discourses are found in Matt 5–7, 10, 13, 18, 24–25. Each one ends with the formulaic statement "when Jesus had finished" these words, this instruction, these parables. The Greek formula in each one is the same; *kai egeneto etelesen ho Iesous* (7:28; 11:1; 13:53; 19:1; 26:1).

1995 has sold over sixty-five million copies to date. The concept of the great tribulation sells.

Since the Olivet Discourse has such a large presence in the Gospel record (two whole chapters containing ninety-seven verses), and since so many evangelical Christians are hypnotized by its prophecies of woe (generating best-selling books) , and since, as we will see, it is a valuable tool for apologetics in confirming the integrity of biblical prophecy (showing Christ's ability to prophesy future events), it well deserves our consideration in the Made *Easy* Series.™

Unfortunately, Christ's woeful teaching here is woefully misunderstood. Among the vast majority of evangelicals this passage is as absolutely confused as it is immensely popular. Indeed, the average evangelical approach to the Olivet Discourse is so seriously misconstrued that it places its fulfillment at the wrong place in history, misses Christ's whole point entirely, applies its judgments to the wrong people, and spreads its catastrophes far beyond its intended focus. Thus, the popular conception has the wrong time, purpose, objects, and scope for its judgments. You could not more seriously miss the meaning of a prophecy than through this four-fold failure.

The dominant, popular understanding regarding the Olivet Discourse holds that:
- Jesus is referring to events in the distant future which are to occur at the very end of the Church age, whereas he is actually speaking of events in the lifetime of his original audience at the end of the old covenant age.
- Jesus is prophesying events regarding the future tribulation-era temple, whereas he is actually prophesying the destruction of the first-century temple and the permanent removal of the sacrificial system.
- Jesus is speaking of catastrophes befalling non-Jews who persecute the Jews, whereas he is actually focusing on disasters overwhelming the Jews for rejecting the Messiah.
- Jesus is declaring judgments overwhelming the entire world, whereas he is actually focusing those judgments upon Judea in the land of Israel.

The two interpretations could hardly be farther apart. These two approaches are known as futurism (which teaches that the prophecies lie in our future even today) and preterism (which teaches that the prophecies lay in the first century).

Of course at this stage of our study I have only *asserted* the error of the popular evangelical approach to Olivet. It will be my task in this book to *prove* it. So then, in this work I will be demonstrating that Jesus gives his famous prophecy as a warning to his original audience regarding the coming destruction of the temple as God judges the first-century Jews living in the land of Israel for rejecting him as their Messiah.

Context Involving Olivet

As noted above, the interpretation of the Olivet Discourse which applies it to Israel's first-century judgment is called "preterism." This theological term derives from the Latin *preteritus*, which means "gone by, past."[2] The evangelical preterist sees many important New Testament prophetic passages as being fulfilled in the early centuries of the Christian era, thus in our own past. Most of these transpired in the era surrounding the AD 70 destruction of the Jewish temple.

The preterist impulse arises *exegetically* from the New Testament text itself. It is sparked by various words or phrases that point to near term expectations: "near," "soon," "speedily," "this generation," "some of those who are standing here shall not taste of death until," and so forth. Having discovered such texts, the preterist also begins to notice other indicators that suggest the near-term expectation more subtly. As I will show, Matthew's Gospel is a good example of both types of indications: exegetical (the textual presence of words denoting imminency) and rhetorical (the development of the Gospel storyline anticipating AD 70).

As a major address on Israel's approaching judgment, the Olivet Discourse does not appear in Christ's teaching as a sudden, stray comment. In fact, it is not only subtly *anticipated* throughout each of the Synoptic Gospel records but is specifically *expected* and *prepared* for. Indeed, it appears as a major discourse toward the *end* of the Lord's ministry as a *dramatic climax* to his ministry to Israel.

In that I will focus on Matthew's version of the Discourse (as the most familiar one), I will show how he fits it into his overall presentation of Christ's ministry and message. We must understand that the Gospels are not biographies. In fact, they create an all new literary genre known as "gospel." As New Testament scholar Donald Guthrie notes: "It has to be concluded that there are no adequate parallels to the genre of the gos-

---

[2] *CEOED*, 2:1330.

pels."[3] He continues: "the marked difference between the gospels in this respect and all other biographical works is crucial if we are to appreciate to the full the uniqueness of these works."[4] The gospels are actually highly-selective, theologically-framed, redemptively-motivated, and situationally-informed presentations of the Lord's ministry and message. Allow me to explain.

The Gospels are obviously *selective* for they focus almost wholly on the three-and-one-half year ministry of his thirty-three year long life, thereby leaving huge gaps in his life. And even then they disproportionately concentrate on one week of his life leading up to and following his death. They are *theological* in that they are designed to show that God sent Christ to fulfill the Old Testament prophecies in order to save men from their sins. They are *motivated* by the desire to encourage faith in and commitment to him who is the Savior of sinners. They are *situational* in that they arise out of the specific historical situations surrounding the apostles in the times when they write them, as we can detect in various rhetorical emphases in them.[5]

Matthew's Gospel is especially well-structured. Indeed, France notes: "all who have studied Matthew's Gospel in detail have been impressed by the care and literary artistry involved in its composition" including its "overall structure . . . with its dramatic development."[6] Gundry even wrote an important commentary titled *Matthew: A Commentary on His Literary and Theological Art* (1982). Because of this we can easily discern in Matthew the enormous redemptive-historical significance of Israel's judgment in AD 70. Again we may helpfully cite France who notes that:

> we hear repeatedly Jesus' condemnation of "this generation" for its failure to recognize God's messengers and to respond to his call (11:16–24; 12:38–45; 16:4; 17:17), culminating in the clear warning that now the rebellion of Israel has gone too far, and that the time for judgment has come (23:29–36), which leads on in its turn to the prediction of the de-

---

[3] Donald B. Guthrie, *New Testament Introduction* (4th ed.: Downer's Grove, Ill.: InterVarsity, 1990), 19.

[4] Donald A. Hagner, *Matthew 1–13* (Dallas: Word, 1993), 245.

[5] See: John Nolland, *The Gospel of Matthew* (NIGTC) (Grand Rapids: Eerdmans, 2005), 43. Leon Morris, *The Gospel according to Matthew* (Grand Rapids: Eerdmans, 1992), 4–5. R. T. France, *The Gospel according to Matthew* (NICNT) (Grand Rapids: Eerdmans, 1987), 21–22.

[6] France, *Matthew*, 21.

struction of the temple (23:37–39; 24:2ff., leading up to 24:34, 'this generation').[7]

France even observes that one of the four "Central Theological Emphases of Matthew" is "the people of God," which includes a focus on "the failure of Israel." Israel's failure is so pronounced that we may discern "a note of finality this time which is particularly pronounced in Matthew's account."[8] In the end Matthew shows how Jesus' ministry "has broken out of the confines of Judaism and in so doing has brought to an end the exclusive privilege of the Jews as the people of God."[9]

Morris agrees: "There can be no doubt that these [kingdom statements] point to a Jewish way of thinking, but no doubt either that this Evangelist looks for them to be fulfilled in the followers of Jesus, not the Jewish nation."[10] As Nolland put its: "There is a huge paradox involved in Jesus, who comes to announce to Israel the restoration of the kingdom, ending his ministry with an alliance of all the Jerusalem leaders and all the Jewish people baying for his blood."[11]

In order to properly introduce the Olivet Discourse, I will briefly survey Matthew's whole record. This is necessary for showing that not only does Christ himself frequently teach about this approaching catastrophe upon Israel, but that Matthew even structures his Gospel so as to strongly emphasize it. Matthew does this both overtly through his recording Jesus' direct and pointed teaching material, as well as subtly through highlighting his various actions and images brought into his storyline.

Early indicators of Israel's demise

Matthew 1. Matthew opens his Gospel by tracing Jesus' genealogy to Abraham, the "father" of the Jews (Matt 3:9; Luke 1:73; John 8:39). As we will see, Matthew will be presenting Jesus as the new Israel, the true Israel of God. Thus, he begins Jesus' story by tracing his genealogy to Israel's own historical source: Abraham.

In fact, Matthew structures the genealogy in a dramatically interesting and rhetorically significant way which he summarizes in 1:17:

---

[7] R. T. France, *The Gospel according to Matthew* (TNTC) (Grand Rapids: Eerdmans, 1987), 51.
[8] France, *Matthew* (NICNT), 38, 50, 51.
[9] France, *Matthew* (NICNT), 18.
[10] Morris, *Matthew*, 4.
[11] Nolland, *Matthew*, 41.

"Therefore all the generations from Abraham to David are fourteen generations; and from David to the deportation to Babylon fourteen generations; and from the deportation to Babylon to the time of Christ fourteen generations."

As Mounce observes, Matthew intentionally arranges the names from Abraham to David to Christ "in groups of fourteen to coincide with the three important stages of Jewish history: the account of God's people leading up to Israel's greatest king; the decline of the nation, ending in Babylonian exile; the restoration of God's people with the advent of the Messiah."[12] France adds: "by organizing that history into a regular scheme of three groups of fourteen generations . . . it indicates that the time of preparation is now complete, and that in Jesus the time of fulfillment has arrived."[13]

Thus, in his opening presentation Matthew highlights Israel's lost glory in her decline from David to the exile, then presents Christ as her new king (Matt 2:2–3; 21:5) and only hope. Indeed, the very opening summary of Jesus' genealogy includes King David along with Abraham: "The book of the genealogy of Jesus Christ, the son of David, the son of Abraham" (Matt 1:1). As we will see in our survey of Matthew she rejects him (cf. Matt 23:37; 27:42), causing him to re-organize the people of God by judging her and calling the Gentiles. Matthew's account of Jesus' genealogy anticipates AD 70 by recapping Israel's history, showing its collapse from the glory days of King David down into the Babylonian exile. Israel's history will collapse once again, but will arise transformed under the new king, Jesus Christ.

McKnight puts the matter thus:

> The most significant place to begin understanding Matthew's polemic with nonmessianic Judaism is his presupposition that God has directed history to consummate it in Jesus Messiah, son of Abraham and son of David (1:1–17; 5:17–20; 21:33–46). For Matthew, the fulfillment of salvation-history takes place in Jesus Christ, and therefore the fulfillment

---

[12] Robert H. Mounce, *Matthew* (NIBC) (Peabody, Mass.: Hendrikson, 1991), 8.

[13] France, *Matthew* (NICNT), 71. See also Norman A. Beck, *Mature Christianity in the 21st Century: The Recognition and Repudiation of the Anti-Jewish Polemic of the New Testament* (Rev. ed.: New York: Crossroad, 1994), 183–84.

of the people of God realizes itself in the new people of God, the church (16:18; 18:17).[14]

We must understand that "Jewish Christianity did not envisage itself as a new religion, but as a true manifestation of Judaism."[15] Evans adds: "Early Christians did not view themselves as belonging to a religion that was distinct from Judaism. New Testament Christianity was Judaism — that is, what was believed to be the true expression of Judaism."[16]

Matthew 2. In Matthew 2:3 the Apostle reports that men from the east come to worship Jesus, while "all Jerusalem [the capital of Israel and the holy city of the Jews] was troubled" at the news. Thus, Matthew includes the story of Herod to show that "in this narrative the Jews and their king are ranged against the infant Jesus, but Gentiles do him homage."[17] This requires that his parents flee with him to Egypt from where they eventually return. This involves re-enacting in Jesus' life the story of Israel's bondage to Egypt and her deliverance into the Promised Land (Matt 2:13–23). This subtly portrays Israel as a new Egypt, the enemy of God's people, and Jesus as "the true Israel."[18]

Since "all Jerusalem was troubled" this anticipates the holy city's hostility to Jesus which comes to full expression later in Matthew's story (e.g., Matt 16:21; 20:17–19; 23:37; 27:20, 25, 63–64). Gundry notes of this first reference to Jerusalem: "Matthew brings in Jerusalem as the center of antagonism toward Jesus."[19] Thus, early on in his commentary Matthew is preparing us for the Lord's rejection by the Jews and his acceptance by the Gentiles (represented here by "men from the east"; cp. Matt 8:11). Thus, we will begin hearing Matthew's steadily growing drumbeat announcing Jerusalem and Israel's approaching judgment.

Matthew 3. In chapter three Matthew introduces us to the first record of preaching in his Gospel by Jesus' forerunner John the Baptist who

---

[14] Scot McKnight in Craig A. Evans and Donald A. Hagner, *Anti-Semitism and Early Christianity: Issues of Polemic and Faith* (Minneapolis: Fortress, 1993), 62.

[15] McKnight in Evans and Hagner, *Anti-Semitism and Early Christianity*, 56. See also: J. D. G. Dunn, *Unity and Diversity in the New Testament: An Inquiry into the Character of Earliest Christianity* (Philadelphia: Westminster, 1977), 235–66.

[16] Craig A. Evans, in Evans and Hagner, *Anti-Semitism and Early Christianity*, 11.

[17] France, *Matthew* (NICNT), 34.

[18] France, *Matthew* (NICNT), 86.

[19] Robert H. Gundry, *Matthew: A Commentary on His Literary and Theological Art* (Grand Rapids: Eerdmans, 1982), 27

introduces him to Israel. The first words we hear of out of John's mouth are foreboding: "Repent, for the kingdom of heaven is at hand" (Matt 3:1). These are also Jesus' first words in his ministry, as recorded by Matthew: "Repent, for the kingdom of heaven is at hand" (4:17). John and Jesus are confronting Israel with her sin and calling her to repent.

In Matthew 3:8 John warns just before Christ's ministry begins that they need to "bring forth fruit in keeping with repentance." Later we will discover that Israel does not bring forth the fruit of repentance, for Jesus acts out prophetic curse against fruitless Israel (21:19) and declares that he will seek another nation to bear the proper fruit (21:43).

John anticipates Israel's rejection in Matthew 3:9–12 where he rebukes Israel's leaders for boasting that Abraham is their father (3:9). This strongly contrasts Jesus' legitimate claim to Abrahamic descent (Matt 1:1). Indeed, stones are more likely to become God's people than hardhearted Israel (3:9; cp. Luke 19:40; see also: Eze 11:19; 36:26). By recording this statement Matthew is preparing the way for a "radical rethinking of what it means to be the people of God" which comes to strong expression at Matthew 8:10–12.[20]

John warns that "the axe is already laid at the root of the trees" (Matt 3:10), an image of divine judgment (Isa 10:15–19, 33–34; Eze 31; Dan 4:14). Turner notes that the adverb "already" and the present-tense verb "is being laid" strongly depict a "present process. As the kingdom message is preached, those who reject it are already being marked out for judgment, even though the full force of that awful judgment has not yet been felt." Consequently, "immediacy and certainty are implied."[21] As Morris expresses it, "John regards the destruction as inevitable" and the assault is "imminent."[22] Nolland agrees.[23] This matches well with Olivet's statement regarding the nearness of the events, as we shall see.

That the axe is laid "at the root" powerfully teaches that God will not simply prune Israel; he will cut her down at the root. Indeed, regarding Jesus, John declares (shifting his metaphors): "He who is coming" has a "winnowing fork is in His hand, and He will thoroughly clear His threshing floor; and He will gather His wheat into the barn, but He will burn up the chaff with unquenchable fire" (Matt 3:12). This anticipates AD 70 (cp.

---

[20] France, *Matthew* (NICNT), 319.
[21] David L. Turner, *Matthew* (BECNT) (Grand Rapids: Baker, 2008), 114.
[22] Morris, *Matthew*, 60.
[23] Nolland, *Matthew*, 145.

8:10–12; 22:7; cf. 7:16–20). In fact, Luke 13:6–9 records a parable of Jesus that reflects this same concern. Jesus speaks of his three and one-half year ministry to fruitless Israel which is presented as a fig tree. There Jesus declares: "for three years I have come looking for fruit on this fig tree without finding any. Cut it down! Why does it even use up the ground?" (Luke 13:7). Later in Matthew 21 we will see Jesus' prophetic theater in cursing the fig tree (see below: Matt 21:18–19).

Unfortunately, "John's title, 'the Baptist', can obscure what was in fact the main thrust of his ministry, an announcement of the imminent judgment of God and of the coming of the 'greater one'."[24]

Growing evidence for Jesus' turning from Israel

Matthew 4. In this chapter we see Jesus finally beginning his formal ministry after being baptized. After hearing of John's imprisonment he "withdrew into Galilee" (Matt 4:12). This indicates his retreat under pressure so that "certainly we are to see here a renewal of the threat posed to the infant Jesus in 2:1–23."[25] This withdrawal is "a matter of political wisdom" in "view of John's conflict with [King Herod] Antipas."[26] This indicates that "for Matthew, Israel's dark political prospects were symptomatic of her need for the redemption from sin available through Jesus the Messiah."[27]

Interestingly, Jesus' removal to Galilee under these conditions fulfills a prophecy anticipating *Gentile* salvation. Here Matthew cites Isaiah 9:1: "The land of Zebulun and the land of Naphtali, / By the way of the sea, beyond the Jordan, Galilee of the Gentiles — / The people who were sitting in darkness saw a great light" (Matt 4:15–16a).[28] Not only does the verse mention the Gentiles particularly, but as Morris observes "the people" here "seems to be wider than that to one nation," thereby involving the Gentiles.[29]

Thus, we may not only discern a negative portrayal of Israel in this early re-positioning of Jesus' ministry, but the prospect of hope for the Gentiles. Nolland notes this "foreshadowing the extension of the gospel

---

[24] France, *Matthew* (NICNT), 89
[25] Nolland, *Matthew*, 169.
[26] France, *Matthew* (NICNT), 140
[27] Turner, *Matthew*, 133.
[28] See: Nolland, *Matthew*, 173.
[29] Morris, *Matthew*, 82n.

to the Gentiles."[30] France agrees that this "gives a further hint of the direction which [Matthew's] story will develop until the mission which will be launched from Galilee in 28:16 is explicitly targeted at 'all nations' (28:19)."[31] Gundry concurs: "The description of Galilee as 'of the Gentiles' provides the key point in the quotation. . . . This description makes that ministry prefigure his disciples' wider mission to Gentiles."[32] This eventually becomes the message of the New Testament and the experience of Christian history.

Jesus' first recorded words in his preaching to Israel reflect those of John the Baptist: "From that time Jesus began to preach and say, 'Repent, for the kingdom of heaven is at hand'" (Matt 4:17). Here then, "Jesus calls on them to realize that they are unfit for the kingdom of heaven and to repent accordingly. . . . We should not overlook the importance of this call to repentance at the very beginning of Jesus' ministry; everything else follows form that."[33] Given the identity of Jesus' words with John's, we should surmise that they *both* anticipated God's approaching judgment in AD 70 (cf. 3:10–12). Thus, "the immediately striking thing about a first reading of v. 17 has to be the repetition by Jesus of the message of John the Baptist: Jesus proclaims in the north the message that had been silenced in the south."[34]

Matthew 5–7. In the Sermon on the Mount (Matt 5–7), his first major discourse recorded by Matthew, Jesus makes several statements that highlight Israel's negative condition and approaching doom. In the Beatitudes opening the Sermon, he anticipates suffering for his followers — suffering to arise from within Israel:

> Blessed are those who have been persecuted for the sake of righteousness, for theirs is the kingdom of heaven. Blessed are you when men cast insults at you, and persecute you, and say all kinds of evil against you falsely, on account of Me. Rejoice, and be glad, for your reward in heaven is great, for so they persecuted the prophets who were before you. (5:10–12)

---

[30] Nolland, *Matthew*, 173.
[31] France, *Matthew* (NICNT), 143.
[32] Gundry, *Matthew*, 60.
[33] Morris, *Matthew*, 83.
[34] Nolland, *Matthew*, 174.

Here the familiar theme of Israel resisting God by attacking her own prophets appears for the first time in Matthew (cp. 21:35–36; 23:37). This is a common charge in Scripture.[35]

In this Sermon Jesus compares the Jews to the Gentiles (Matt 5:47; 6:7, 32), rather than favorably distinguishing Israel over them. In his statement on the narrow and broad gates he is warning that the current situation in Israel is that "many" are entering the broad gate to destruction and "few" are finding it (7:13–14). In the final analysis the crowds recognize Jesus' superior authority to their own scribes, their most prominent religious authorities (7:28–29).

Matthew 8. As I note above, Matthew has Jesus' public ministry to Israel (Matt 10:6; 15:24) opening by his calling her to repentance. In Matthew 8:10–12 we read of the faithful Gentile who exercises more faith than anyone in Israel. We hear once again of people from the east. This time they sit with Abraham, Isaac, and Jacob (the rightful place of the Jews), while the Jews themselves are cast out in suffering. These will not simply gather crumbs from the table (15:27), but will actually recline as guests at the table with the patriarchs of Israel.

The casting out of the Jews into outer darkness to endure weeping and gnashing of teeth (Matt 8:12) certainly points to God's ultimate judgment. But it also directly pictures the AD 70 judgment when God horribly judges Israel and removes her temple forever. That judgment is a harbinger of the final judgment itself.

Matthew 9. In Matthew 9:16–17 Christ teaches that the constraints of Judaism are like old wineskins that are ready to burst. God, however, will provide new wineskins (the new covenant church) to contain the wine of the kingdom. By this illustration Jesus explains that he "was not simply bringing in a revised and updated Judaism, or even founding a new sect within Judaism. What he was teaching and doing were such that they could not be contained within the accepted Jewish system. . . . His new approach could not be fitted into those old forms."[36] Thus, "the gospel cannot be added to Judaism."[37]

---

[35] 1Kgs 18:13; 19:1, 10, 14; 2Ch 24:19–21; Neh 9:26; Jer 2:30; 26:20–24; Matt 5:12; 21:35–36; 23:37; Luke 11:47; 13:33; Acts 7:52; Rom 11:3; 1 Thess 2:15; Heb 11:36–37.
[36] Morris, *Matthew*, 226–27.
[37] Hagner, *Matthew 1–13*, 245.

Matthew 10. At Matthew 10:5 Jesus emphatically limits his personal ministry to Israel: "Do not go in the way of the Gentiles." By this he is providing an opportunity for Israel to repent (as per his opening message in Matthew at 4:17), though ultimately they will not (Matt 23:37; cp. 11:20–21, 41). Thus, in Matthew 10:16–17 he warns that the Jewish synagogues will punish his followers: "Behold, I send you out as sheep in the midst of wolves; therefore be shrewd as serpents, and innocent as doves. But beware of men; for they will deliver you up to the courts, and scourge you in their synagogues."

So then, in Matthew 10:23 he promises that he will soon judge Israel: "Whenever they persecute you in this city, flee to the next; for truly I say to you, you shall not finish going through the cities of Israel, until the Son of Man comes." This "coming" is a metaphor that "refers to the coming of the Son of Man in judgment in the destruction of Jerusalem in A.D. 70."[38] A few verses later (Matt 10:34–36) he warns that he has not come to bring peace on the earth (i.e., "the Land" of Israel), but a sword which will divide homes among the Jews (cp. 10:34–36).

Matthew 11. In Matthew 11:14 Christ declares that John the Baptist fulfills the prophecy of Elijah's return: "And if you care to accept it, he himself is Elijah, who was to come." France notes that here Jesus explicitly identifies John the Baptist with the Elijah prophecy of Malachi. This means that:

> if the forerunner has already come and finished his work, presumably "the great and terrible day of the Lord" for which Elijah was to prepare the way is now here. Perhaps it is the startling christological implications of this claim which explain the uncharacteristically coy tone of the opening clause, "if you are willing to accept it." To accept that John is the returning Elijah is to embrace a whole package of eschatological fulfilment in Jesus for which clearly most of those who heard him were not yet ready — cf. the unresponsiveness of "this generation" which will be condemned in vv. 16–19.[39]

Jesus states that "this generation" is rejecting both his and John the Baptist's ministries:

> To what shall I compare this generation? It is like children sitting in the market places, who call out to the other children, and say, "We played the flute for you, and you did not dance; we sang a dirge, and you did

---

[38] Hagner, *Matthew* (NICNT), 280.
[39] France, *Matthew* (NICNT), 432.

not mourn." For John came neither eating nor drinking, and they say, "He has a demon!" The Son of Man came eating and drinking, and they say, "Behold, a gluttonous man and a drunkard, a friend of tax-gatherers and sinners!" Yet wisdom is vindicated by her deeds. (Matt 11:16–19)

Jesus rebukes and warns cities in Israel of God's judgment, comparing them unfavorably to wicked Old Testament cities:

> Then He began to reproach the cities in which most of His miracles were done, because they did not repent. "Woe to you, Chorazin! Woe to you, Bethsaida! For if the miracles had occurred in Tyre and Sidon which occurred in you, they would have repented long ago in sackcloth and ashes. Nevertheless I say to you, it shall be more tolerable for Tyre and Sidon in the day of judgment, than for you. And you, Capernaum, will not be exalted to heaven, will you? You shall descend to Hades; for if the miracles had occurred in Sodom which occurred in you, it would have remained to this day. Nevertheless I say to you that it shall be more tolerable for the land of Sodom in the day of judgment, than for you." (Matt 11:20–24)

Once again France is helpful:

> Even in Galilee, including Jesus' 'own' town of Capernaum, the honeymoon period is apparently over And when those who have been privileged to witness Jesus' ministry in their own communities fail to respond, they must expect to face a more serious judgment than the notorious pagan cities which had no such special revelation.[40]

Thus, Matthew's Gospel again presents a negative comparison of Israel over against Gentiles.

As Hagner points out: "Now the extent of the rejection of Jesus comes into full light. With the unbelief of Israel, a turning point in the narrative has been reached."[41] Israel will not repent; her judgment will be severe.

Matthew 12. In Matthew 12:39 he characterizes Israel of his day as an "evil and adulterous generation." So then in 12:41 he once again rebukes and warns Jewish cities of God's coming judgment. But this time he compares them to Nineveh which did repent by responding favorably to God's preaching through Jonah.

After another unfavorable comparison of Israel to Gentiles (here the "Queen of the South," Matt 12:42), in Matthew 12:44–45 the apostle

---

[40] France, *Matthew* (NICNT), 437.
[41] Hagner, *Matthew*, 313.

draws an analogy that speaks of the seven-fold demonization of Israel at the end of "this evil generation." Hagner observes:

> This evil generation (cf. v 39) had experienced the powerful deeds of Jesus, which included demon exorcism, and to that extent had benefitted. But there had been no repentance, no acceptance of and commitment to Jesus and his cause, and thus this generation would be as susceptible to the power of evil as ever; indeed, the judgment it would later experience would be far worse than when Jesus began his ministry In view . . . may be the destruction of Jerusalem (cf. 24:2, 15) and not simply eschatological judgment.[42]

Matthew 13–15. In Matthew 13:58 we read that the Lord performs few miracles in his home town (13:54) due to their lack of faith. In Matthew 15:7–14 he rebukes the rabbis in Israel for neglecting God's word and teaching falsely, according to Isaianic prophecy.

Final proof of Israel's recalcitrance and rejection

Matthew 16. In Matthew 16:4 Jesus once again speaks of Israel as an evil and adulterous generation. And at v 21 he warns his disciples that Israel's religious leaders — even her "chief priests" (which included past and present high-priests of God's temple!) — will kill him. Not only so, but we must note something quite remarkable here. In Matthew Jesus never mentions Jerusalem until he states he is going there to be killed by its leaders. This becomes even more significant in that Matthew himself never mentions Jesus' several visits to Jerusalem until he shows him entering it to die (21:1). Yet we know from John's Gospel that the Lord did visit there often, even very early in his ministry (John 2:23; 5:1; 7:25; 10:22–23; 12:12–14). But Matthew (and Mark) bypasses that information as he builds his case against Jerusalem and Israel.

As a consequence of the religious leaders killing him, he teaches in 16:28 that some of his followers will live to see him "coming in his kingdom" (Mark reads that they will "see the kingdom of God after it has come *with power*," Mark 9:1). In that only "some of those standing here" will live to see it, this must point to the AD 70 destruction of the temple which occurs forty years later.

Premillennial scholar Alford explains that this statement refers to :
> *the destruction of Jerusalem*, and the full manifestation of the Kingdom of Christ by the annihilation of the Jewish polity; which event, in this aspect

---

[42] Hagner, *Matthew*, 357.

as well as in all its terrible attendant details, was a *type* and *earnest* of the final coming of Christ. . . . The fact is, there is a reference back in this discourse to that in ch. x., and the *coming* here spoken of is the same as that in ver. 23 there.[43]

Matthew 17. In Matthew 17:10–13 Jesus declares that John the Baptist fulfills the Elijah prophecy (Mal 4:5). He also laments that the Jews did not recognize him as such and that their leaders killed him, just as they will kill Jesus. In this context Jesus once again declares the first-century Jews to be an evil generation, but this time even more strongly: they are an "unbelieving and perverted generation" (Matt 17:17). Their evil condition is exacerbated by the fact that they reject Christ even though they are witnesses to what "many prophets and righteous men desired to see . . . and hear" (13:17; cp. John 8:56; Heb 11:13; 1 Pet 1:10–12).

Matthew 19. Matthew 19:28 dramatically presents Jesus promising his disciples: "Truly I say to you, that you who have followed Me, in the regeneration when the Son of Man will sit on His glorious throne, you also shall sit upon twelve thrones, judging the twelve tribes of Israel."

By "regeneration" Jesus speaks of the great change from the old covenant economy to the new. John Calvin notes: "I would rather relate 'regeneration' to Christ's first coming, for it was then that the world began to be renewed and the Church emerged from death's darkness into the light of life."[44] Gill agrees, noting that the "regeneration" means:

> the new state of things, in the church of God, which was foretold, and is called the time of reformation, or setting all things right, which began upon the sealing up the law, and the prophets, and the ministry of John the Baptist, and of Christ; who both, when they began to preach, declared, that this time, which they call the kingdom of heaven, was at hand, just ushering in. . . . This new dispensation is called the regeneration.[45]

---

[43] Henry Alford, *Alford's Greek Testament: An Exegetical and Critical Commentary* (7th. ed.: Oxford University Press, 1874),1:177.

[44] John Calvin, *A Harmony of the Gospels: Matthew, Mark and Luke*, trans. by T. H. L. Parker (Grand Rapids: Eerdmans, 1972), 2:262.

[45] John Gill, *Exposition of the New Testament* (London: Mathews and Leigh, 1809), 1:219.

Matthew Henry concurs: "The time of Christ's appearing in this world was a time of regeneration, or reformation (Heb. ix. 10), when old things began to pass away, and all things to look new."[46]

This could signify God's people being reconstituted as the new covenant Church, so that the Church takes over the role of "the twelve tribes of Israel." If so, "judging" would simply mean "ruling, leading." Thus, the New Israel (the Church) will have new leaders: the Christ-commissioned apostles who bring God's new covenant revelation. According to Albright and Mann: This is "an assertion of the new creation, the new age, to be inaugurated by the exaltation of The Man . . . Jesus promises that when the new age of the Messiah is inaugurated in his passion and exaltation, the disciples will share in the administration of the Kingdom."[47]

Though this idea of "regeneration" is undoubtedly correct, the great Hebraist John Lightfoot offers a better explanation of Jesus' point. He explains that the:

> thrones set up . . . are not to be understood of the last judgment of Christ, but of his judgment in his entrance upon his evangelical government, when he was made by his Father chief ruler, king, and the judge of all things . . . [Consequently, this pictures] the judgment of Christ to be brought upon the treacherous, rebellious, wicked, Jewish people.[48]

Henry allows a similar meaning (as one option among other things in this multi-layered statement):

> When Christ appears for the destruction of Jerusalem (*ch.* xxiv. 31), then shall he send the apostles to judge the Jewish nation, because in that destruction their predictions, according to the word of Christ, would be accomplished.[49]

This verse presents the persecuted apostles (Matt 10:16–18) as the ones who will get the last word against their persecutors in Israel (10:19–20; 16:28). That is, as they faithfully preach Christ and as Israel sinfully continues to reject him, they will effectively secure and oversee Israel's

---

[46] Matthew Henry, *Matthew Henry's Commentary on the Whole Bible* (Old Tappan, N. J., Revell, rep. n.d.), 5:279.

[47] W. F. Albright and C. S. Mann, *Matthew* (AB) (Garden City, N.Y.: Doubleday, 1971), 234.

[48] John Lightfoot, *Commentary on the New Testament from the Talmud and Hebraica* (Peabody, Mass.: Hendrickson, 1989 [rep. Oxford University Press, 1859]), 1:266.

[49] Henry, *Commentary*, 5:2880.

judgment in AD 70 — as anticipated in Matthew 10:23 and in several other references in Matthew and many places in the New Testament.

Matthew 20. In this chapter we learn that Christ once again prophesies that the religious leaders of Israel (including their chief priests) will condemn him to death, then deliver him over the Gentiles to crucify him (Matt 20:17–19). He is not painting a pretty picture of Israel's first-century spiritual condition and moral conduct.

Matthew 21. I am tracing Matthew's highly-structured presentation of Jesus' ministry to show how it anticipates the Olivet Discourse in Matthew 24–25. In 21:1f Jesus enters Jerusalem (for the first time in Matthew's Gospel; see discussion at 16:21). Jerusalem is the capital of Israel, the home of God's temple, the seat of the high priesthood and their religious rule over Israel.

Matthew is clearly organizing his material to emphasize Jesus' climactic entry into Jerusalem to confront and rebuke Israel's religious authorities. As noted above this confrontation has been brewing since 16:21: "From that time Jesus Christ began to show His disciples that He must go to Jerusalem, and suffer many things from the elders and chief priests and scribes, and be killed, and be raised up on the third day" (cp. 20:18).

Now that we are entering into Matthew 21, we must recognize, as France points out, that Olivet is the climax of 21:23–23:39 which presents Christ in the temple. He dramatically enters the temple in 21:12–16 and equally dramatically leaves it in 24:1.[50] Another oddity in Matthew's presentation is that he *never* mentions Jesus even going near the temple until he enters it to cast out the moneychangers (21:12ff). In John's Gospel, however, John mentions the Lord's appearing there frequently, even at the very beginning of his ministry (John 2:14–15; 5:14; 7:14, 28; 8:2, 20; 10:23; 18:20).

Jesus carefully orchestrates his public entry in Jerusalem by securing a donkey to ride on (Matt 21:1–7) in fulfilment of prophecy (21:5; cp. Zech 9:9). He seems to be accepted by the common people as they spread their garments before him and cry out: "Hosanna to the Son of David; / Blessed is He who comes in the name of the Lord; / Hosanna in the highest!" (21:9). However, only part of their accolade comes from Scripture (Psa 118:26). The other part betrays their nationalistic and political expectations as they add to the Psalm reference: "Hosanna to the Son of David." We see that this proclamation does not represent a deep

---

[50] France, *Matthew* (NICNT), 886.

commitment, for not long afterwards the chief priests and elders persuade the multitudes to ask for Barabbas to be released rather than Jesus (Matt 27: 20–21). They then scream to Pilate: "Let Him be crucified" (27:22–23).

At Matthew 21:12–13 Jesus enters the temple and casts out the moneychangers and overturns their tables. This is not directed solely at the moneychangers and sellers (and through them the religious authorities who oversee their activities). Rather it also a rebuke of *all* who have come to the temple to worship, for Matthew notes that he "cast out *all* those who were *buying* and selling in the temple" (21:12). That is, he is casting out worshipers who are "buying" the sacrificial animals so that they might offer them in worship. The temple has become something contrary to God's design. By this action Christ is rejecting "the whole system of sacrificial worship."[51]

This activity is what scholars call "prophetic theater," a purposely acted out prophecy.[52] As Nolland well observes: This "seems to be yet another instance of prophetic symbolism. The other temple texts to which it perhaps has some relationship are the prophecy of the temple's doom in 24:1–2 (cf. v. 15) and the accusation against Jesus in 26:61; 27:40."[53] As Wright expresses it: "Jesus not only predicted its destruction, buy symbolized it in his prophetic action, commonly called its 'cleansing.'"[54] Jesus is here symbolically acting out the overthrow of the temple in AD 70.

We may see that Jesus intends his actions as prophetic theater by the following: (1) He could not have been attempting to put a final stop to all the merchandising activity, for one man could not stop the whole enterprise in the enormous temple. Yet Jesus acted alone and did not even call upon his disciples to assist him. (2) We do not read of him coming back to the temple to see that it was no longer operating, nor do we read of his taking any further action against it.

(3) Jesus specifically quotes a verse from a famous passage in Jeremiah: "My house shall be called a house of prayer" (Matt 21:13; cp. Jer 7:11).

---

[51] France, *Matthew* (TNTC), 786.
[52] See Old Testament examples of prophetic theater: Isa 20; Jer 13:1-11; 19; 27:1-15; 32; 43:8-13; Eze 4:1-3; 4:4-8; 4:9-17; 5:1-54; 12:1-16; 12:17-20; 37:15-28.
[53] Nolland, *Matthew*, 844.
[54] Chris Wright in Peter W. L. Walker, ed., *Jerusalem Past and Present in the Purposes of God* (2d ed.: Grand Rapids: Baker, 1994), 11.

In its original context this verse is a part of God's denunciation of the Old Testament temple and his warning of its coming destruction (Jer 7:1, 13–15, 20) despite Israel's confidence in it (Jer 7:4).[55] (4) When the chief priests and elders demand to know by what authority Jesus does this (Matt 21:15–16), he directly links himself back to John the Baptist who prophesies Israel's coming judgment (Matt 21:23–26; cp. 3:1, 7–12). (5) Matthew seems to confirm this by the next action Jesus undertakes just seven verses after his "cleansing" — when he curses the fig tree (21:18–19). (6) Not much later he will declare the temple desolate (Matt 23:38) and announce its coming destruction (24:2).

So then, in Matthew 21:19–21 Jesus curses the fig tree and speaks of the mountain being thrown in the sea. The curse on the fig tree is certainly "an acted symbol of judgment to come on Jerusalem."[56] Otherwise, it would be an uncharacteristic, vindictive display of destructive power by Christ. This action seems to reflect Micah's lament of Israel's lack of fruit, of the absence of godly persons in the Land (Mic 7:1–2). In fact, Jesus gives a fig tree parable expressing the same truth in Luke 13:6–9 which summarizes his three-and-one-half year ministry to fruitless Israel. The Lord's curse symbolically warns that Israel "has reached a point of no return."[57]

This whole cursing of the fig tree is surprising as we may discern from Mark's version. Mark specifically notes that "when He came to it, He found nothing but leaves, *for it was not the season for figs*" (Mark 11:13). This alerts us to the fact that Jesus' desire was not ultimately to find food. He was making a dramatic point about Israel's fruitlessness and her coming judgment. The Lord frequently states in his ministry: "He who has ears, let him hear" (Matt 11:15; 13:9, 43). His disciples must carefully consider what he is doing here — not long after denouncing the temple and all of its worshipers. Before long he will give a parable about how Israel was nurtured by God but failed to produce fruit (see below at

---

[55] Oftentimes when Old Testament prophecies are cited in the New Testament they are evoking the whole original context. This literary practice is called metalepsis. In antiquity the Scriptures were not divided into chapters and verses, so that metalepsis was the means whereby a writer could point readers to the fuller contexts of a passage.
[56] France, *Matthew* (NICNT), 792.
[57] France, *Matthew* (NICNT), 794.

21:33ff) and how God will take the kingdom from her and give it "to a nation producing the fruit of it" (21:43).

The casting of the mountain into the sea probably refers to the destruction of the temple. Hooker notes of Mark's parallel account (Mark 11:23), that this mountain "may well have been understood by Mark as a reference to the temple mount. . . . Mark has here reminded us that the withered fig tree and the action in the temple have the same significance."[58] Gray agrees: "Just as the withered tree was a symbol of the temple's fate, so too the mountain cast into the sea reaffirms Jesus' condemnation of the temple."[59] Wright well notes that "anyone using this language while standing in the vicinity of the Mount of Olives and looking towards the city could only mean one thing, especially in the first century," i.e. the temple mount.[60] Though Scripture can speak proverbially of moving mountains (Isa 40:4; 45:2; 49:11; Zech 4:7), here in Jerusalem Jesus is being more specific for he is referring to "*this* mountain" (Matt 21:21).

After this Matthew records a series of parables and vigorous dialogues between Jesus and Israel's religious authorities: the chief priests (Matt 21:15, 23, 45), scribes (21:15; 23:2, 13ff), elders (21:23), Pharisees (21:45; 22:41; 23:13ff), Herodians (22:15–16), and the Sadducees (22:23–24). His three warning parables in 21:28–22:14 clearly show his denunciation of Israel's leaders and their coming judgment.

In Matthew 21:28–32 we read the parable of the two sons. This parable sets up a demeaning contrast between the religious leaders and the outcasts of Jewish society. The second son represents the religious authorities who claim to be obedient to the father but who are not (v 30). The first son represents "the tax-gatherers and harlots" (v 31) who will enter God's kingdom before "you," i.e., the chief priests (v 31–32, cp. v 23). Once again Jesus highlights the failure of Israel's leaders (cp. 3:7–10; 12:38–42; 15:1–7).

In Matthew 21:33–45 Jesus presents the parable of the landowner. In this parable the landowner obviously represents God, and his vineyard

---

[58] Morna D. Hooker, *Gospel according to St. Mark* (BNTC) (Peabody, Mass.: Hendrickson, 1991), 269.

[59] Timothy C. Gray, *The Temple in the Gospel of Mark: A Study in Its Narrative Role* (Grand Rapids: BakerAcademic, 2010), 52.

[60] T. Wright in Peter W. L. Walker, ed., *Jerusalem Past and Present in the Purposes of God* (Grand Rapids: Baker, 1994), 63.

pictures Israel (Isa 5:7; cp. Isa 5:1ff; Psa 80:8; Jer 12:10). The "tower" pictures the temple, in both Isaiah 5:2 and Matthew 21:33 (cp. Mic 4:8). The landowner carefully prepares his vineyard, then rents it out to vine-growers (Israel's leaders) expecting to receive from its produce (its fruit).

When the time for its harvest comes, the owner sends his "slaves" (Gk.: *doulos*) to receive his produce. These represent the prophets who are called God's *douloi* ("servants") in the Old Testament (1 Kgs 18:13, 22–27; 2 Chr 24:21; 36:15–16; Neh 9:26; Amos 3:7; Zech 1:6).[61] But the vine-growers kill them. Then he sends his son, only to have the vine-growers kill him. This indisputably speaks of the religious authorities of Israel killing Jesus (cp. Matt 16:21; 20:18) for at the end Matthew informs us: "And when the chief priests and the Pharisees heard His parables, they understood that He was speaking about them" (21:45).

According to Jesus' own interpretation this shows that God will take his kingdom from the Jews, resulting in their being crushed:

> "Therefore I say to you, the kingdom of God will be taken away from you, and be given to a nation producing the fruit of it. And he who falls on this stone will be broken to pieces; but on whomever it falls, it will scatter him like dust." And when the chief priests and the Pharisees heard His parables, they understood that He was speaking about them. (Matt 21:43–45)

This is all based on the theological fact that God owns "the Land" (Lev 25:23) and dwells therein (Num 35:34). Therefore "land and righteousness are inextricably linked."[62] Thus, when Israel rebels against God, her Land will be judged (Lev 20:22–26; 26:14–43; Deut 4:25–27; 28:15–68). God will take the kingdom from Israel and give it to "a nation" that will produce fruit. The word for "nation" is singular, not plural. It speaks of a new "holy nation" (1 Pet 2:9), the international church which Jesus establishes (Matt 16:18).

Matthew 22. In Matthew 22:1–14 Jesus presents the parable of the king (God) who gives a wedding feast for his son (Jesus). Those originally invited (the Jews; Matt 10:5; 15:24) refuse to come (they do not accept Jesus as the Messiah). As a consequence, "the king was enraged and sent

---

[61] Israel is notorious for killing her prophets: 1 Kgs 18:13; 19:1, 10, 14; 2 Chr 24:19–21; Neh 9:26; Jer 2:30; 26:20–24; Matt 5:12; 21:35–36; 23:37; Luke 11:47; 13:33; Acts 7:52; Rom 11:3; 1 Thess 2:15; Heb 11:36–37.

[62] Gary M. Burge, *Jesus and the Land: The New Testament Challenge to "Holy Land" Theology* (Grand Rapids: Baker: 2010), 6.

his armies, and destroyed those murderers, and set their city on fire" (Matt 22:7). This speaks of the Romans burning Jerusalem in AD 70.

Matthew 23. In this chapter Jesus utters seven woes upon the Pharisees who "have seated themselves in the chair of Moses" (they have a leadership role over Israel through their interpretation of the Mosaic law). After issuing these woes, in Matthew 23:32–36 he warns that first-century Israel will "fill up then the measure of the guilt of your fathers" by persecuting his followers "from city to city" so "that upon you may fall the guilt of all the righteous blood shed on the earth." (Note Paul's similar statement at 1 Thess 2:14–16.)

At the end of this long denunciation, the Lord dogmatically states: "Truly I say to you, all these things shall come upon *this* generation" (Matt 23:36). This is obviously pointing to AD 70. This statement reappears again in Matthew 24:34. Since Matthew 23 establishes the specific context of the Olivet Discourse, I will deal with it more fully in my next chapter.

Matthew 26. Skipping the Olivet Discourse (Matt 24–25), which will be the focus of the bulk of *Olivet Discourse Made Easy*, we come to Matthew 26:3–5. Here Israel's chief priests and elders along with the high priest counsel Jesus' death. They begin implementing their evil plan in 26:14–15 where they pay Judas to betray Jesus to them (cp. 26:21–25, 45).

In Matthew 26:47 the "chief priests and elders of the people" come with Judas to arrest Jesus. The Lord rebukes Peter for taking up a sword to defend Jesus by warning: "Put your sword back into its place; for all those who take up the sword shall perish by the sword" (26:52). This instructs the disciples that such actions are incompatible with his message (cp. 5:39–42) and against God's will for his death (26:2, 53–54; John 18:11). But it also probably warns of what will befall Israel as they take up the sword against Rome in AD 66. This action eventually leads to the full-scale Jewish War which destroys Jerusalem and the temple (AD 66–70). Jesus warns of this earlier in Matthew 10:34 (cf. 10:23; cp Luke 22:36–38).

In Matthew 26:57 the arresting party hauls Jesus before Israel's highest court, a meeting of the Sanhedrin consisting of the high priest, scribes, and elders. There he undergoes trial before the high priest who even attempts to present false witnesses against him (26:59). Prominent in his trail are the reports of his denouncing the temple, though his words are twisted by false-witnesses: "This man stated, 'I am able to destroy the temple of God and to rebuild it in three days'" (26:61).

In Matthew 26:64 Jesus warns that the high priest himself along with the Sanhedrin will see him coming in cloud-judgment against them: "Jesus said to him [*auto*, sing.], 'You [*su*, sing.] have said it yourself; nevertheless I tell you [*humin*, pl.], hereafter you shall see [*opsesthe*, pl.] the Son of Man sitting at the right hand of Power, and coming on the clouds of heaven.'"

France well captures the meaning and significance of this statement:

> The 'coming on the clouds of heaven' cannot be read as a reference to the *parousia*, as has been the traditional exegesis until relatively recently. See on 24:30 for a parallel issue, where exactly the same words are used . . . with reference . . . to the enthronement of the Son of Man in contrast to the destruction of the temple. There the event predicted was to take place within 'this generation' [cf. Matt 24:34], and here, too, Matthew's wording demands a fulfillment which is imminent rather than set in the indefinite future: it is something which 'you' (the current Sanhedrin members) 'will see,' and it will come true 'from now on' . . . . In the vindication of the repudiated Messiah and in the powerful growth of the movement which they have attempted to suppress, they 'will see' that it is he who is now seated on the heavenly throne.[63]

I would note that the NASB's "hereafter" is based on the Greek *ap arti*, which is literally translated "from now," which means from this point in time.

In Matthew 26:65 the high priest declares Jesus blasphemes, and as a consequence he tears his high-priestly robes. This not only signifies his judgment but also prefigures the coming rending of the temple veil (Matt 27:51) at Jesus' death on the cross (which is only mentioned in Matthew's Gospel) and the ultimate destruction of the temple itself. Then the Sanhedrin spit on him and beat, slap, and taunt him (26:67–68).

Matthew 27. In Matthew 27:1 "all the chief priests" discuss with the "elders of the people" how to kill Jesus. In vv 11–12 Jesus appears before the Roman procurator Pilate where the chief priests and elders accuse him. In vv 15–21 when Pilate tries to release Jesus, the chief priests resist him: "but the chief priests and the elders persuaded the multitudes to ask for Barabbas, and to put Jesus to death" (27:20). When Pilate attempts again to release him, "they kept shouting all the more, saying, 'Let Him be crucified'" (27:22).

---

[63] France, *Matthew* (NICNT), 1027–28.

Finally Pilate declares himself innocent of Christ's blood (Matt 27:24), to which the people respond: "And all the people answered and said, 'His blood be on us and on our children!'" (27:25). Then, while he is dying on the cross the people and the leaders mock him one last time:

> And those passing by were hurling abuse at Him, wagging their heads, and saying, "You who are going to destroy the temple and rebuild it in three days, save Yourself! If You are the Son of God, come down from the cross." In the same way the chief priests also, along with the scribes and elders, were mocking Him, and saying, "He saved others; He cannot save Himself. He is the King of Israel; let Him now come down from the cross, and we shall believe in Him." (27:39–42)

Matthew 28. In Matthew 28:11–15 the chief priests assemble after Jesus' resurrection to bribe the Roman guards at his tomb, directing them to claim that his disciples stole his body. So finally as Matthew's Gospel closes, Jesus appears and gives his Great Commission. In this Commission he commands his followers to take the gospel to "all nations" (28:19), rather than limiting their ministry to Israel as previously (10:16–17; 15:24). God is turning from the Jews to the world.

Conclusion

This brief survey of Matthew's Gospel is important for setting the literary and historical context of the Olivet Discourse with its warning of Israel's judgment in AD 70. Both Jesus' repeated teaching and actions, as well as Matthew's overall historical flow and literary presentation clearly highlight God's approaching wrath upon Israel. This understanding of Matthew is so clear as to be undeniable. In fact, Lowery — though a dispensationalist — can even speak of "the strong denunciation of Israel that pervades the gospel" employing a "strong polemic against Israel."[64]

This disturbing presentation of Israel's spiritual condition and historical expectation is so obvious, strong, frequent, and widespread in the New Testament that many liberal historians and theologians (wrongly) charge the New Testament itself as the ultimate source of anti-Semitism in the world.[65] For instance, Dandmel dogmatically states that "the New

---

[64] David K. Lowery, in Donald K. Campbell and Jeffrey L. Townsend, eds., *A Case for Premillennialism: A New Consensus* (Chicago: Moody, 1992), 166, 171.

[65] See especially: John Dominic Crossan, *Who Killed Jesus? Exposing the Roots of Anti-Semitism in the Gospel Story* (San Francisco: HarperSanFrancisco, 1995). Dan Cohn-Sherbok, *The Crucified Jew: Twenty Centuries of Anti-Semitism* (Grand Rapids:

Testament is a repository for hostility to Jews and Judaism.... Christian Scripture is permeated by it."[66] Galambush (an apostate Christian) states that 1Thessalonians 2:14–16 "was slanderous in its original context and, in later years, disastrous in its consequences."[67] Beck meticulously researches the entire mass of New Testament assertions against the Jews. He highlights anti-Judaic verses, even urging re-translating the New Testament to remove them.[68]

This negative evaluation of the New Testament in general applies to Matthew's Gospel in particular. Jewish scholar Flusser comments on Matthew 8:11–12 regarding the "sons of the kingdom" being cast out: "This is a vulgar anti-Judaism of many members of the early Gentile church."[69] Gaston warns that "there is a great deal in Christian theology which needs to be rethought after Auschwitz, and one good place to begin is with Matthew."[70] Regarding the infamous statement in Matthew 27:25, Galambush laments: "It is hard to imagine a more anti-Jewish account than this 'most Jewish' gospel."

This is a naive reading of the New Testament's polemical critique of Israel. Ancient rhetoric was far more vigorous than in our overly-sensitive modern world of political-correctness. Jesus himself employs insulting epithets, calling the scribes and Pharisees "hypocrites" (Matt 23:13, 15, 23, 25, 27, 29), a "son of hell" (23:15), "blind guides" (23:16, 24)," "blind

---

Eerdmans, 1992). T. A. Burkill, "Anti-Semitism in St. Mark's Gospel," New Testament 3 (1959): 34–52. W. R. Farmer, *Anti-Judaism and the Gospels* (Harrisburg, Penn.: Trinity, 1999). Riemund Bieringer, Didier Pollefeyt, and Frederique Vandecasteele, eds., *Anti–Judaism and the Fourth Gospel* (Louisville, Kent.: Westminster John Knox, 2001). L. T. Johnson, "The New Testament's Anti-Jewish Slander and the Conventions of Ancient Polemic," *Journal of Biblical Literature* 108 (1989): 419–41.

[66] Samuel Sandmel, *Anti-Semitism in the New Testament?* (Philadelphia: Fortress, 1978), 160.

[67] Julie Galambush, *The Reluctant Parting: How the New Testament's Jewish Writers Created a Christian Book* (San Francisco: HarperSanFrancisco, 2005), 125; cf. 59.

[68] Norman A. Beck, A. *Mature Christianity in the 21st Century: The Recognition and Repudiation of the Anti-Jewish Polemic of the New Testament* (rev. ed.: New York: Crossroad, 1994).

[69] David Flusser, *Judaism and the Origins of Christianity* (Jerusalem: Magness, 1988), xxiii.

[70] Lloyd Gaston, "The Messiah of Israel as Teacher of the Gentiles: The Setting of Matthew's Theology," *Interpretation* 29: (1975): 39.

men" (23:17, 19), "fools" (23:17), and "serpents . . . brood of vipers" who deserve hell (23:33). He accuses them of ostentatious religiosity (23:5–6), shutting people out of the kingdom of God (23:13), robbery and self-indulgence (23:25). Indeed, they are nothing but "dead men's bones and all uncleanness" (23:27), and murderers of the prophets (23:31).

But rather than being anti-Semitic diatribes, this language is stereotypical rhetoric that was widely-used by the Jews themselves in inter-party squabbles. Davies and Allison list many parallels between Jesus' long denunciation in Matthew 23 and ancient Jewish practice.[71] Not only so, but this sort of strong invective was employed by the Old Testament prophets. Indeed, Isaiah 5:8–23 almost seems to be Jesus' model.

As evangelical Christians we must recognize the redemptive-historical significance of Matthew's strong message against Israel. This is exactly what Israel's own Bible, our Old Testament, warns about when she rebels against God:

> But it shall come about, if you will not obey the Lord your God, to observe to do all His commandments and His statutes with which I charge you today, that all these curses shall come upon you and overtake you . . . . The Lord will bring a nation against you from afar, from the end of the earth, as the eagle swoops down, a nation whose language you shall not understand, a nation of fierce countenance who shall have no respect for the old, nor show favor to the young. . . . And it shall besiege you in all your towns until your high and fortified walls in which you trusted come down throughout your land, and it shall besiege you in all your towns throughout your land which the Lord your God has given you. . . . And it shall come about that as the Lord delighted over you to prosper you, and multiply you, so the Lord will delight over you to make you perish and destroy you; and you shall be torn from the land where you are entering to possess it. (Deut 28:15, 49–50, 52, 63)

This is not anti-Semitism; it is biblical covenantalism.

---

[71] W. D. Davies and Dale C. Allison, Jr., *The Gospel according to Saint Matthew* (ICC) (Edinburgh: T & T Clark, 1988), 3: 3:258–61. For example, the Dead Sea Scrolls were written by a hyper-orthodox Jewish sect (the Essenes) who withdrew from Jerusalem in despair over the corruption of the priesthood, cult, and temple. Their polemic against Israel is downright vicious.

Chapter 2
OLIVET'S SPECIFIC IMPETUS
Matthew 23

In the previous chapter I surveyed Matthew's whole Gospel to show that it continually highlights Israel's failure, anticipates her judgment, and gradually demonstrates God's turning from her to the Gentiles. This is Matthew's *general* setting for the Olivet Discourse. Jesus' fateful Discourse is not a violent intrusion breaking unexpectedly into Matthew's otherwise placid scene of Jesus' ministering to Israel. Rather, it is anticipated from the Gospel's very opening words.

In Matthew 2:3 "all Jerusalem" was troubled at the news of Jesus' birth. In Matthew 23:37 Jesus weeps over Jerusalem: "O Jerusalem, Jerusalem, who kills the prophets and stones those who are sent to her! How often I wanted to gather your children together, the way a hen gathers her chicks under her wings, and you were unwilling." By the time we arrive at 23:37 which leads into the Discourse, "a negative image of Jerusalem is already anticipated in 2:3; 16:21; 20:18."[1] As a consequence of all of this, Matthew's Gospel ends with a Commission to "all the nations" (Matt 28:19).

My Current Focus

What I will do in this chapter is narrow our Matthew study to the *immediate* historical context of the Olivet Discourse. This will explain the *particular* circumstances that directly sparked Christ's strong message about the Temple's final doom. Before I begin I will cite France's insightful comments from his smaller Matthew commentary in the Tyndale New Testament Commentary series. Here he briefly summarizes Matthew's flow leading up to the Discourse.

> We hear repeatedly Jesus' condemnation of 'this generation' for its failure to recognize God's messengers and to respond to his call (11: 16–24; 12:38–45; 16:4; 17:17), culminating in the clear warning that now the rebellion of Israel has gone too far, and that the time for judgment has

---

[1] John Nolland, *The Gospel of Matthew* (NIGTC) (Grand Rapids: Eerdmans, 2005), 950.

come (23:29–36), which leads on in its turn to the prediction of the destruction of the temple (23:37–39; 24:2ff.). . . .

Where this comes to the fore is chapters 21–23, where Matthew has brought together a variety of sayings and incidents which together add up to a clear repudiation of the official leadership of Israel. Jesus' demonstration in the temple and his symbolic cursing of the fig-tree (Matthew emphasizes the *immediacy* of the effect), the challenge to Jesus' authority and his deliberate endorsement of John the Baptist's ministry of warning, the sequence of three polemical parables, which add up to a scathing indictment of the nation's failure to produce 'fruit' and the threat of replacement by 'another nation,' the series of theological and other debates in which Jesus progressively worsts his opponents (22:46), after which they remain silent throughout chapter 23 while he ruthlessly exposes their 'hypocrisy' and expresses God's repudiation of their empty worship, and warns that the long-delayed judgment must now fall — all this amounts to a powerful climax to the confrontation which has built up throughout the Gospel.[2]

Let us now focus on Matthew 23 to see what finally sparks the warning against Israel that we find in Matthew 24.

The Olivet Discourse is recorded in each of the three Synoptic Gospels: Matthew 24–25; Mark 13; and Luke 21. Matthew provides his own distinctive approach to the Lord's sermon. For instance, preceding the Discourse, the Gospels of Mark and Luke provide only very brief warnings regarding the hypocrisy of the scribes (Mark 12:38–39; Luke 22:45–47). Matthew, however, provides a much lengthier denunciation of these religious authorities, along with the Pharisees: 23:1–38. Because of this France can note: "When we come in Matthew to Jesus' prediction of the destruction of the temple, the ground has been well prepared; Jerusalem's rejection of its last chance to repent means that 'your house is left to you deserted' (23:36–38)."[3] As Turner puts it: "the judgment of Jerusalem is justified in Matt. 23 before it is predicted in Matt. 24–25."[4] France agrees in his introduction to Matthew 23: "the ground has been well prepared; Jerusalem's rejection of its last chance to repent means that 'your house is left to you deserted' (23:36–38)."

---

[2] R. T. France, *The Gospel according to Matthew* (TNTC) (Grand Rapids: Eerdmans, 1987), 51–52.

[3] R. T. France, *The Gospel of Matthew* (NICNT) (Grand Rapids: Eerdmans, 2007), 853.

[4] David L. Turner, *Matthew* (BECNT) (Grand Rapids: Baker, 2008), 544.

The basic structure of this important chapter is as follows: In Matthew 23:1–12 Jesus speaks to the crowds (23:1) regarding corruption among "the scribes and Pharisees" (23:2). Later in verses 13–36 he speaks directly to the scribes and Pharisees themselves, uttering seven woes against them. Then in 23:37–39 Matthew himself provides a bridge from these two sections into the Olivet Discourse itself.

As we will see Matthew 23 is intricately related to chapter 24. As Gibbs puts it: "the two discourses run together as one." But contrary to some scholars it is not a part of the Discourse itself; rather it is a segue to it. Both the location of Jesus and his audiences change: In Matthew 24 Jesus leaves the temple to go to the Mount of Olives (24:1, 3); and he no longer speaks to the multitudes or the scribes and Pharisees (23:1) but to his disciples (24:3).

This chapter is important in building Matthew's climax. Jesus' confrontations with the religious leaders rapidly intensify in chapters 21–22, where we see him personally debating them and giving parables about them. Thus, "Matt. 23 [is] the culmination of Jesus's confrontations with Jerusalem's religious leaders that began in 21:15."[5] But in chapter 23 he turns to a direct frontal assault on them in their role as religious authorities. He first warns the crowds about their hypocrisy, then levels seven woes directly against them. By rebuking Israel's leaders he shows her corporate failure as the people of God. As he states earlier the problem is: "they are blind guides of the blind. And if a blind man guides a blind man, both will fall into a pit" (Matt 15:14).

We will learn in this chapter that "Israel's rejection of God's messengers through the ages has now reached a point of no return."[6] The storm clouds have gathered, the crack of doom is sure. And soon.

Jesus' Warnings to the Jewish People

The Lord's castigation of Israel's religious authorities, the scribes and Pharisees, is significant regarding his warning to Israel about the coming destruction of the temple (Matt 24:2ff). He opens his message "to the multitudes" (23:1):

> The scribes and the Pharisees have seated themselves in the chair of Moses; therefore all that they tell you, do and observe, but do not do

---

[5] Turner, *Matthew*, 543.
[6] France, *Matthew*, 853.

according to their deeds; for they say things, and do not do them. (Matt 23:2–3; cp. Matt 5:20)

Here he accepts their *formal* legitimacy as interpreters of God's Law. After all, such a function in Israel is important for God's people to whom he gave his Law to guide them (Deut 4:1–24; 7:1–11). But he rejects the way they have handled that vital role.

We should probably understand his call in Matthew 23:3a (to do "all that they tell you") as tongue-in-cheek sarcasm. We know that he cannot literally mean to do this because of the word "all." How could he urge his followers to follow "all" they teach? After all, throughout his ministry he criticizes their interpretations of the Law (e.g., Matt 6:1–18; 9:11–13; 12:1–8; 15:1–20; 16:6–12; 12:1–14; 19:3–9). As noted above he previously called them "blind guides of the blind" (15:14). In fact, he will repeat this charge several times just a few verses later (23:16, 17, 19, 24, 26).

Besides all of this, in the very next verse Jesus criticizes their teaching as oppressive: "they tie up heavy loads, and lay them on men's shoulders; but they themselves are unwilling to move them with so much as a finger" (Matt 23:4). This is contrary to his own teaching which offers an easy yoke and a light load (11:30; cp. Acts 15:10, 28; 1 John 5:3) even though he himself promotes God's Law (Matt 5:17–20).

Jesus charges these teachers of the Law with ostentatious displays of religiosity: they "do all their deeds to be noticed by men" and proudly display their badges of spirituality (Matt 23:5). In his own teaching, however, Jesus repeatedly urges humility (23:11–12; cp. 11:29; 18:3–4; 20:26–27). His followers must be discrete, giving alms in secret (6:2–4) and praying secretly rather than on street corners (6:5–7). Israel's religious leaders have transformed God's holy worship to prideful displays.

In addition to the obvious moral and spiritual implications of Jesus' call to humility, we should recognize very important historical and practical aspects as well. In Matthew 23:12 he states that "whoever exalts himself shall be humbled; and whoever humbles himself shall be exalted." As with many of his teachings, this statement has an "eschatological orientation."[7] Their prideful boasting will be judged on judgment day at the end of history. But in addition this seems also to highlight the approach-

---

[7] W. D. Davies and Dale C. Allison, Jr., *The Gospel according to Saint Matthew* (ICC) (Edinburgh: T & T Clark, 1988), 3:279.

ing AD 70 judgment (which also is eschatological, being a pointer to the final judgment). Let me explain.

As Jesus notes (Matt 23:6–7), the scribes and Pharisees exercise a prominent role in the life and culture of Israel. But in AD 70 God will so terribly judge Israel that these proud religious authorities will have their world turned upside down and twisted inside out. Turner well captures the implication of Jesus' statement: "Jesus's disciples have humbled themselves and will be exalted. The leaders' vain attempt to exalt themselves over God's Messiah will result in their being humbled."[8]

The Pharisees (John 11:47) actually fear their being humbled from their position of power and privilege. But they thought it would occur if they *failed* to judge Jesus, for they warn the Sanhedrin: "If we let Him go on like this, all men will believe in Him, and the Romans will come and take away both *our place* and our nation" (John 11:48). By this statement we should understand "the concern of the rulers, accordingly, was primarily for their own position, not for the temple and the people."[9]

Therefore, we must understand Jesus' statement in Matthew 23:12 as involving a warning regarding AD 70 for the following reasons: (1) His teaching in Matthew 21–22 makes several allusions to this looming judgment (21:12, 19, 21, 41, 43–45; 22:7, 13). (2) This call to humility corresponds with earlier calls in Matthew 3:2–12; 8:10–12; and 19:28–30, each of which anticipates AD 70. (3) This statement is one element in his building the case against Israel regarding God's soon-coming judgment, as we will see in Matthew 23:32–38. (4) Matthew 23 is introducing Matthew 24 (cp. 23:38 with 24:1, 16) which speaks of the temple's destruction (24:2).

Jesus' Rebuke of the Jewish Authorities

At Matthew 23:13 Jesus begins directly addressing the scribes and Pharisees. Here he starts levying seven woes against them (Matt 23:13, 15, 16, 23, 25, 27, and 29).[10] He strongly declares their teaching false and their influence dangerous.

Throughout Matthew we learn that Jesus has come preaching the "kingdom of heaven": "From that time Jesus began to preach and say,

---

[8] Turner, *Matthew*, 548.
[9] George R. Beasley-Murray, *John* (Dallas: Word, 1989), 196.
[10] Matt 23:14 is textually precarious, not being found in the earliest Greek manuscripts.

'Repent, for the kingdom of heaven is at hand'" (Matt 4:17; cp. 5:3, 10, 19–20; 7:21; 10:7; 11:12; 13:1ff; etc.). But here at 23:13 he rebukes Israel's religious teachers because they "shut off the kingdom of heaven from men." Indeed, they themselves "do not enter in . . . nor do [they] allow those who are entering to go in." They are using their religious authority as teachers of God's Law to resist Jesus' teaching, even though he is their Messiah, "the Christ, the Son of the living God" (Matt 16:16).

Judaism enjoyed much growth through securing proselytes, as we see in Scripture (e.g., Matt 23:35; Acts 2:10; 6:5; 13:43) and elsewhere.[11] Regarding Israel's first century experience, the noted Jewish scholar Louis Feldman speaks of "the outstanding success of Jewish proselytism."[12] But Jesus laments that when the scribes and Pharisees make a proselyte they "make him twice as much a son of hell as yourselves" (Matt 23:15). Therefore, the scribes and Pharisees are "blind guides" and "fools" (23:16, 17) who are leading the Jews to destruction.

While the wrath of God is brewing against Israel, their leaders worry about meticulously tithing "mint and dill and cummin" — and this while they "have neglected the weightier matters of the law: justice and mercy and faithfulness" (Matt 23:23). Once again he rejects them as "blind guides" who are leading the people in the wrong direction (23:24). They are punctilious in keeping themselves ceremonially clean for public show, but inside "they are full of robbery and self-indulgence" (23:25). Remember: Jesus rejects the temple they control as a den of "robbers" (21:13) and the Jews choose a "robber" over Jesus (John 18:40).

Thus, spiritually the scribes and Pharisees are like "whitewashed tombs" which are "full of dead men's bones and all uncleanness" (Matt 23:27). Their religiosity is all vain show and hollow spirituality. They not only are spiritually dead themselves but also "bear witness against" themselves that they "are sons of those who murdered the prophets" (23:31). This reminds them that Israel has a long history of killing God's prophets (1 Kgs 19:10; Neh 9:26; Jer 2:30; 26:20–24; etc.). Not only so but it links

---

[11] Judith 14:10; Josephus, *Antiquities*, 20:2:1 §1–5; Philo, *Abraham*; Justin, *Dialogue with Trypho the Jew*, 80, 122ff; Tacitus, *Histories* 5:5; Dio, *Roman History* 57: 18: 5; Horace, *Satires* 1:4:141–44.

[12] Louis H. Feldman in Hershel Shanks, ed., *Christianity and Rabbinic Judaism: A Parallel History of Their Origins and Early Development* (Washington, D.C.: Biblical Archaeology Society, 1992), 5.

back to Jesus' reference to his forerunner, the "prophet" John the Baptist, whom they also rejected (21:25–27).

Jesus' reference to their history of killing the prophets is designed to warn them of the danger they face. He is reminding them that their first temple was destroyed despite the earnest appeals of God's prophets whom Israel violently rejected. In 2 Chronicles 36:15–16 we read:

> And the Lord, the God of their fathers, sent word to them again and again by His messengers, because He had compassion on His people and on His dwelling place; but they continually mocked the messengers of God, despised His words and scoffed at His prophets, until the wrath of the Lord arose against His people, until there was no remedy.

As a result the Babylonians "burned the house of God, and broke down the wall of Jerusalem and burned all its fortified buildings with fire, and destroyed all its valuable articles" (2 Chr 36:19).

In the context of Jeremiah's warning about the first temple's destruction (Jer 7:4, 14–15, 20, 34) that prophet declares the same truth as the writer of 2 Chronicles:

> Since the day that your fathers came out of the land of Egypt until this day, I have sent you all My servants the prophets, daily rising early and sending them. Yet they did not listen to Me or incline their ear, but stiffened their neck; they did evil more than their fathers. (Jer 7:25–26)

Thus, Jesus is following the pattern of Jeremiah and the writer of 2 Chronicles as he prepares Israel for the destruction of her second temple: "Fill up then the measure of the guilt of your fathers" (Matt 23:32). The idea of "filling up" the measure of sin appears frequently in Scripture (Gen 15:16; Dan 8:23; 9:24; 1 Thess 2:14–16; cp. 2 Macc 6:14). By this statement the Lord indicates that at that moment they have not finally filled up their rebellion. But soon they will crucify Christ and persecute his followers.

Stephen is stoned to death (Acts 7:54–60) for making this very point in his sermon: "Which one of the prophets did your fathers not persecute? And they killed those who had previously announced the coming of the Righteous One, whose betrayers and murderers you have now become; you who received the law as ordained by angels, and yet did not keep it" (7:52–53).

Now once again, Christ links his message of soon-coming judgment with John's prophetic witness: "You serpents, you brood of vipers, how shall you escape the sentence of hell?" (Matt 23:33). We read of John's almost identical statement just before Jesus begins his ministry: "But when he saw many of the Pharisees and Sadducees coming for baptism, he said to them, 'You brood of vipers, who warned you to flee from the wrath to come?'" (3:7).

Though Israel has a long history of killing her prophets and though the scribes and Pharisees are "sons of those who murdered the prophets" (Matt 23:31), nevertheless Jesus will send more prophets to confront them. Israel's violence against them will finally bring about God's judgment for all their rebellious history:

> Therefore, behold, I am sending you prophets and wise men and scribes; some of them you will kill and crucify, and some of them you will scourge in your synagogues, and persecute from city to city, that upon you may fall the guilt of all the righteous blood shed on earth, from the blood of righteous Abel to the blood of Zechariah, the son of Berechiah, whom you murdered between the temple and the altar. (Matt 23:34–35)

This warning of Israel's violent reaction against Jesus' followers appears previously in Matthew's record (e.g., 10:16–23; 21:33–36).

We know this points to AD 70 because the next verse expressly declares: "Truly I say to you, all these things shall come upon this generation" (Matt 23:36). Jesus continually warns that first-century generation of Israel regarding their enormous sin (11:16; 12:39, 41–42; 16:7; 17:7).

Now Matthew presents:

Jesus' Bridge to the Olivet Discourse

Here in Matthew 23:37–39 Jesus makes his final public appeal to Israel, but laments that they will not listen and that they are therefore doomed:

> O Jerusalem, Jerusalem, who kills the prophets and stones those who are sent to her! How often I wanted to gather your children together, the way a hen gathers her chicks under her wings, and you were unwilling. Behold, your house is being left to you desolate! For I say to you, from now on you shall not see Me until you say, "Blessed is He who comes in the name of the Lord!"

His statement "O Jerusalem, Jerusalem . . . *how often* I wanted to gather your children together" clearly indicates he has frequently visited Jerusalem. *Yet Matthew only mentions this one visit just before his crucifixion.* As I noted previously John's Gospel records several visits (John 2:23; 5:1; 7:25; 10:22–23; 12:12–14). But Matthew only mentions Jesus' last visit just before his death: he does this in order to dramatically build his climax regarding Israel's approaching judgment.

Jesus' mention of the temple is particularly ominous. He refers to the temple as "*your* house." Though as recently as Matthew 21:13 he cites a Scripture that calls the temple "*My* house." Thus, it is no longer "My house" but "your house."[13] In fact, the structure of Jesus' sentence strongly emphasizes his rejecting the house as no longer God's house, but theirs. He does not simply say: "I am leaving your house desolate." Rather the Greek sentence reads literally: "Behold, is left *to you* the house *of you* desolate." Furthermore, this seems intentionally intended to reflect God's statement to Jeremiah: "I have forsaken My house, / I have abandoned My inheritance; / I have given the beloved of My soul / Into the hand of her enemies" (Jer 12:7).

Almost immediately after this statement, we read of Jesus' leaving the temple for the last time: "And Jesus came out from the temple and was going away" (Matt 24:1a). His only reference to the temple from this point forward is to announce its destruction (24:2ff). Then in the Olivet Discourse which follows he picks up on the term "desolate" (*eremos*) in 23:38 by stating in 24:15: "Therefore when you see the abomination of *desolation* [*eremoseos*] which was spoken of through Daniel the prophet, standing in the holy place."

Before entering into his judgment discourse, however, the Lord makes a statement that is frequently misunderstood. It is often lifted out of its context to make a point which is the very opposite of his intention. That statement reads: "For I say to you, from now on you shall not see Me until you say, 'Blessed is He who comes in the name of the Lord!'" (Matt 23:39). Upon first reading this declaration appears to offer a positive, future hope for Israel. When read in its context, though, it leaves the opposite impression. Let me briefly explain.

Elsewhere Scripture promises the ultimate, worldwide victory of the gospel — which will include widespread conversions of racial Jews (e.g., Rom 11:11–12, 15, 25–26).[14] But Matthew's presentation of Jesus' statement does not point to that eventuality. Rather what Jesus is here pro-

---

[13] Interestingly Stephen uses this same sort of pronoun shift in his sermon against the Sanhedrin in Ac 7. There he identifies himself as a Jew by speaking of "our father[s]" (7:2, 11, 15, 19, 32, 38, 39, 44–45). But then he shifts his statement when condemning the Jews: he finally declares them to be "your fathers" (7:51–52).

[14] For this optimistic eschatology, known as postmillennialism, see my: *Postmillennialism Made Easy* (Draper, Vir.: ApologeticsGroup, 2010).

phesying is Israel's *constrained admission* of Jesus' blessedness because they reject him. The reasons for this interpretation are as follows[15]:

(1) The opening word "for" is the Greek connective *gar*. This strongly connects the statement with Jesus' preceding negative pronouncement: "your house is being left to you desolate" (Matt 23:38). He had just lamented that he had often tried to gather them, but they "were unwilling" (23:37). (2) The phrase "until you say" is a condition of *indefinite* possibility. It does not affirm that Israel *will in fact* bless Christ.

(3) The whole flow of chapters 23 and 24 militates against any positive prospect. Jesus has just stated that Israel will fill up the measure of guilt of their fathers (Matt 23:32), persecute his followers (23:34), answer for the guilt of righteous blood (23:35), finally reject him (23:37), and experience the abandonment of their temple (23:38). Then in the next chapter he gives his long judgment discourse warning about the temple's absolute destruction (23:2), its coming "abomination of desolation" (24:15), the necessity of his followers fleeing from Jerusalem and Judea (24:16), and his judgment coming against "the tribes of the land" (24:29–30).

Thus, Israel will not "see" Jesus again until they are constrained under his judgment to recognize who he is.[16] That is, at AD 70 they will "see" (i.e., realize) that he is the Son of Man.[17] This is the type of seeing that Jesus refers to in Matthew 26:64: "Jesus said to him, 'You have said it yourself; nevertheless I tell you, hereafter you shall see the Son of Man sitting at the right hand of Power, and coming on the clouds of heaven.'"

Conclusion

The Gospel writers do not simply select stray stories and remembrances and stitch them together in a patchwork quilt. They are literary artists carefully weaving their narratives in such a way as to present a beautiful tapestry of redemptive-historical truth.

---

[15] My presentation is based on France's, *Matthew* (TNTC), 332–33.

[16] We read of sinners' constrained praise of Christ on judgment day in Rom 14:11 and Phil 2:10.

[17] The concept of "seeing" here does not imply a literal seeing. After all, Jerusalem does literally see him again when they reject him at his trial (Matt 26:20, 25) and mock him on the cross (26:39–44, 47, 49) — which certainly are not the sort of seeing to which he here refers.

Throughout his Gospel Matthew prepares us well for the Olivet Discourse. We have noted that Matthew has especially prepared us for this discourse by his narrative in 21:12–23:39, particularly in chapter 23. We will see that this famous sermon strongly focuses on God's judgment upon Israel at the destruction of Jerusalem and the temple in AD 70. With all the preceding introduction in chapters 1 and 2 above, we are now ready to enter into the Olivet Discourse itself.

Chapter 3
OLIVET'S CENTRAL FOCUS
Matthew 24:1–3

The first three verses in Matthew 24 are not actually part of the Olivet Discourse, but rather serve to set it up more pointedly than even Matthew 23. Matthew is tightening the screws on Israel. In these important verses we read:

> And Jesus came out from the temple and was going away when His disciples came up to point out the temple buildings to Him. And He answered and said to them, "Do you not see all these things? Truly I say to you, not one stone here shall be left upon another, which will not be torn down." And as He was sitting on the Mount of Olives, the disciples came to Him privately, saying, "Tell us, when will these things be, and what will be the sign of Your coming, and of the end of the age?" (Matt 24:1b-3).

The central focus of the Olivet Discourse is divine judgment. In the earlier portion we read of God's judgment upon Israel, including her temple (Matt 24:2, 15), holy land (24:16), messianic expectations (24:5, 23–24), and people ("tribes," 24:30). Then Christ links her judgment thematically to the final judgment of the world (24:36–51). Following that he adds two parables regarding the last judgment (25:1–30, 31–46).

In Matthew 24:1a Jesus ceremoniously leaves the temple: "Jesus came out from the temple and was going away." He has just declared it "desolate" (23:38), now he acts out her truly desolate condition by personally leaving it and "going away," never again to return to it. This ends his public ministry for he states: "you will not see Me until" (23:39).

Many commentators note that Matthew's dramatic presentation has Jesus reenacting, as it were, God's forsaking of the temple in the Old Testament in the context of its first judgment. We read in Ezekiel 11:23: "And the glory of the Lord went up from the midst of the city, and stood over the mountain which is east of the city." That mountain "east of the city" would be the Mount of Olives (Zech 14:4). Here in Matthew Jesus heads there (Matt 24:3) in order to give his sermon on the temple's destruction (24:2) and desolation (24:15).

The Temple's Imposing Glory

As Jesus departs the temple "His disciples came up to point out the temple buildings to Him" (Matt 24:1b). Matthew does not inform us why they point out the buildings to him. But apparently they are surprised that Jesus has rejected the temple in that they appear to deem it a beautiful monument to God's glory and a worthy place of worship. We may gather this both exegetically and historically.

Exegetically, we find in Mark 13:1b a fuller presentation of the disciples' comment: "Teacher, behold what wonderful stones and what wonderful buildings." Thus, they are specifically pointing out the magnificent glory of its structure. Jesus replies: "Do you see these great [*megalas*] buildings?" (Mark 13:2a).

Historically, we know from ancient reports that the Herodian temple with its enormous stones and magnificent buildings was truly breathtaking, enjoying fame throughout the Roman world. Roman historian Tacitus notes that the Jewish temple "was famous beyond all other works of men" and was a "temple of immense wealth" (*Hist* 5:8). Later rabbis proudly declared that "he who has not seen the temple in its full splendor has never seen a beautiful building" (*b. Sukk* 51b).

Josephus is our main eyewitness to the majesty of the temple.[1] A few select statements highlight the temple's beauty and size:

> Now the temple was built of stones that were white and strong, and each of their length was twenty-five cubits, their height was eight, and their breadth about twelve. . . . [Herod] also encompassed the entire temple with very large cloisters, contriving them to be in a due proportion thereto; and he laid out larger sums of money upon them than had been done before him, till it seemed that no one else had so greatly adorned the temple as he had done. (*Ant* 15:11:3 [392, 396])
>
> • • •
>
> [Of one of the temple buildings he states that the] front was all of polished stone, insomuch that its fineness, to such as had not seen it, was incredible, and to such as had seen it, was greatly amazing (*Ant* 15:11:5 [416]).
>
> • • •
>
> Now the outward face of the temple in its front wanted nothing that was likely to surprise either men's minds or their eyes; for it was covered

---

[1] For the full Josephan description see: *Ant* 15:11:3, 5 (392–402; 410–20); *J.W.* 5:51–5 (184–226). See also: Tacitus, *Hist* 5:8.

all over with plates of gold of great weight, and, at the first rising of the sun, reflected back a very fiery splendor, and made those who forced themselves to look upon it to turn their eyes away, just as they would have done at the sun's own rays. But this temple appeared to strangers, when they were coming to it at a distance, like a mountain covered with snow; for as to those parts of it that were not gilt, they were exceeding white. On its top it had spikes with sharp points, to prevent any pollution of it by birds sitting upon it. Of its stones, some of them were forty-five cubits in length, five in height, and six in breadth. Before this temple stood the altar, fifteen cubits high, and equal both in length and breadth; each of which dimensions was fifty cubits. (*J.W.* 5:5:6 [222–25]

• • •

It was the most admirable of all the works that we have seen or heard of, both for its curious structure and its magnitude, and also for the vast wealth bestowed upon it, as well as for the glorious reputation it had for its holiness. (*J.W.* 6:4:8 [267]).

The first century Jewish philosopher Philo (25 BC—AD 40) deems the temple "beautiful beyond all possible description." He states that "the buildings of it are of most exceeding beauty and magnificence, so as to be universal objects of admiration to all who behold them, and especially to all foreigners who travel to those parts, and who, comparing them with their own public edifices, marvel both at the beauty and sumptuousness of this one" (*Spec. Laws* 1:13 [72, 73]). He speaks of it as "our most beautiful and renowned temple, which is respected by all the east and by all the west, and regarded like the sun which shines everywhere" (*Embassy* 29 [191]). It is "the most beautiful of all the temples in the world" (*Embassy* 30 [198]).

Even today a portion of the massive foundation platform on which the temple stood still exists. The visible portion is 1600 feet long and 100 feet high. Most of its stones weigh between four and eight tons, though one of them, known as Wilson's Arch, is forty feet long and weighs 570 tons. This whole wall is known to us as the famous "Wailing Wall."

But now Jesus begins speaking about:

The Temple's Coming Destruction

After his disciples point out the majestic temple, Jesus responds: "Do you not see all these things? Truly I say to you, not one stone here shall be left upon another, which will not be torn down" (Matt 24:2). We should be careful to observe his emphasis. Note that he says the same thing twice, using different words, to emphasize the devastation: "not one stone here shall be left upon another." Then he underscores this by re-stating it: "which will not be torn down."

Jesus' warnings of the temple's destruction are apparently widely known to others because they are charged against him twice in Matthew's next few chapters. During his trial the Sanhedrin dredges up false witnesses against him (Matt 26:60). Two of these testify: "This man stated, 'I am able to destroy the temple of God and to rebuild it in three days'" (26:61). Their witness is false in that they state he himself would destroy it, but it is rooted in the truth of his prophesying its destruction.

Then later as he hangs on the cross he is taunted with this altered statement: "You who are going to destroy the temple and rebuild it in three days, save Yourself! If You are the Son of God, come down from the cross" (Matt 27:40). Thus, his teaching against the temple and his warnings of its destruction are so prominent in his teaching that they are used to justify his execution.

Because of the physical enormity of the temple and the Jews' religious confidence that God would not allow his house to be destroyed, Israel assumes the temple was indestructible. Just twenty years before its devastation, Philo comments on the temple's income, using words assuming its perpetual endurance:

> The temple has for its revenues not only portions of land, but also other possessions of much greater extent and importance, which will *never be destroyed or diminished*; for as long as the race of mankind shall last, the revenues likewise of the temple will *always be preserved*, being *coeval in their duration with the universal world*. (*Spec.* Laws 1:14 [76])

This view of the impervious character of the temple is found in other ancient writings. For instance, in the Sibylline Oracles 5:401 (*ca.* AD 100) we read of the destruction of the temple: "the ever-flourishing, watchful Temple of God / made by holy people and hoped / by their soul and body to be always imperishable." Previously during the first temple period Israel makes the same mistake. The Lord warns them through Jeremiah: "Do not trust in deceptive words, saying, 'This is the temple of the Lord, the temple of the Lord, the temple of the Lord'" (Jer 7:4). Israel feels she is safe because of the everlasting temple of God in their midst.

But within one generation of Jesus' prophecy, the Herodian temple lay in absolute ruin, destroyed by the mighty Roman army. Josephus describes the final loss of the temple which fulfilled Jesus prophecy that "not one stone here shall be left upon another, which will not be torn down":

Now as soon as the army had no more people to slay or to plunder, because there remained none to be the objects of their fury, (for they would not have spared any, had there remained any other work to be done,) Caesar gave orders that they should now demolish the entire city and temple, but should leave as many of the towers standing as were of the greatest eminency; that is, Phasaelus, and Hippicus, and Mariamne; and so much of the wall as enclosed the city on the west side. This wall was spared, in order to afford a camp for such as were to lie in garrison, as were the towers also spared, in order to demonstrate to posterity what kind of city it was, and how well fortified, which the Roman valor had subdued; but for all the rest of the wall, it was so thoroughly laid even with the ground by those that dug it up to the foundation, that there was left nothing to make those that came thither believe it had ever been inhabited. This was the end which Jerusalem came to by the madness of those that were for innovations; a city otherwise of great magnificence, and of mighty fame among all mankind." (J.W. 7:1:1 [1–4])

Jesus alludes to this horrific event when he responds to the chief priests and the elders of the people" (Matt 21:23) with these fateful words: "Therefore I say to you, the kingdom of God will be taken away from you, and be given to a nation producing the fruit of it" (21:43). He has this destruction in mind when during his trial he warns the high priest and Sanhedrin: "You have said it yourself; nevertheless I tell you, hereafter you shall see the Son of Man sitting at the right hand of Power, and coming on the clouds of heaven" (26:64). Then in AD 70 the worst fears of the chief priests and Sanhedrin are fulfilled: "If we let Him go on like this, all men will believe in Him, and the Romans will come and take away both our place and our nation" (John 11:48).

The Disciples' Surprised Query

Upon hearing their Lord solemnly declare the temple's coming destruction "the disciples come to Him privately, saying, 'Tell us, when will these things be, and what will be the sign of Your coming, and of the end of the age?'" (Matt 24:3). It is absolutely essential that we note that this is the spark that ignites Jesus' explosive discourse.

As we have been noticing, the temple is the key element in the whole historical setting of the Discourse. Jesus' prophecy of its final destruction (Matt 24:2) follows after his declaring it "desolate" (23:38) and dramatically walking out of it (24:1). What is more, after his originally entering the temple in Matthew 21:12 (the first time Matthew mentions his visiting Jerusalem and the temple) almost all of his activities, interaction, and teaching relate to it. In Matthew's record these include:

- his casting out the moneychangers from the temple (21:12–16)
- his cursing the barren fig tree then explaining that prayer can cast the Temple mount into the sea (21:18–22)
- the chief priests and elders' (21:23) challenge to Jesus demanding the source of his authority for casting the moneychangers out of the temple (21:23–27)
- his response to the chief priests' authority-challenge by offering two parables regarding their failure as Israel's religious leaders (21:28–32, 33–46)
- his parable of the marriage feast picturing the destruction of Jerusalem (22:7), the temple city (22:1–14)
- the Pharisees' plot to entrap him because of "what He said" (22:15–22), followed by the Sadducees' (the main party from which the high priests came) effort to do the same (22:23–33), which was followed once again by an effort from the Pharisees (22:34–45), all of which result in Matthew's conclusion that "no one was able to answer Him a word, nor did anyone dare from that day on to ask Him another question" (22:46)
- his lengthy, scathing rebuke (23:1–36) of the scribes and Pharisees who "have seated themselves in the chair of Moses" (23:2) and are therefore the ones who teach Israel (23:7–8) regarding ritual law governing the temple, including ceremonial cleanness (23:27–28), which rebuke also mentions the temple's gold (23:16–17), altar (23:18), offerings (23:19–20), and tithes (23:23) that were used to support the levitical priesthood (Num 18:21, 24 28)

Clearly, Matthew maintains an intense narrative focus on the temple and Jesus' reaction to the temple. The Olivet Discourse *must* deal with the temple's destruction. *But dispensationalists deny Matthew's presentation of the Discourse even mentions the AD 70 temple destruction.* Their system requirements will not allow it, causing them to badly miss the whole point of Jesus' teaching in Matthew 24. Let me briefly highlight the dispensational error.

Upon hearing Jesus' statement of the temple's coming destruction (Matt 24:2) the disciples' first question regards "when will these things be" (24:3b). At this point Pentecost claims there is an omission in Matthew's record: "The answer to the first question is not recorded by

Matthew, but is given in Luke 21:20–24"! He contends that it is only in those five verses in Luke 21 that we read the "portion of the discourse [that] had to do with the destruction of Jerusalem under Titus in 70 A.D."[2] According to Pentecost the next question is Matthew's only concern: "what will be the sign of your coming, and of the end of the age?" Pentecost states: "The entire passage in Matthew 24 and 25 was written to answer this question concerning the signs of Messiah's coming [i.e., the rapture], which would terminate the age."[3]

This is a standard dispensational practice. For instance, *The Popular Encyclopedia of Biblical Prophecy* agrees with Pentecost: "The disciples' first question in the Olivet Discourse relates to the destruction of Jerusalem in A.D. 70. Christ's answer is recorded only in Luke 21. Matthew 24–25 and Mark 13 deal only with the last question, which refers to events that have not yet occurred."[4] The *Tim LaHaye Prophecy Study Bible* agrees: "the first question is answered in Luke's account and was fulfilled in A.D. 70 (Luke 21:20–24)," whereas "the second question" deals with "the end of the age," involving the rapture, tribulation, and second advent.[5] Price states that "it should be observed that while all three questions are asked in Matthew 24:3 and Mark 13:4, Jesus only answers questions two and three in these contexts."[6]

How could this possibly be? With all the preparation for Israel's coming judgment in his long record, and with his special focus on the temple since chapter 21, why would Matthew skip over the leading question of the disciples? And even drop the matter without any comment or expla-

---

[2] J. Dwight Pentecost, *Things to Come: A Study in Biblical Eschatology* (Grand Rapids: Zondervan, 1958), 276.

[3] Pentecost, *Things to Come*, 276.

[4] Tim LaHaye and Ed Hinson, eds., *The Popular Encyclopedia of Bible Prophecy* (Eugene, Ore.: Harvest, 2004), 249.

[5] *Tim LaHaye Prophecy Study Bible* (Chattanooga, Tenn.: AMG, 2001), 1151. I would note that the editors contradict themselves on the very next page, where they state: "therefore, the entire discourse must be looked upon as answering all three questions" (p. 1152). This contradicts the previous page on two points: (1) by claiming there are three questions, not two; and (2) by claiming that all three questions are answered in Matthew 24:1–25:46.

[6] Randall Price, *The Temple and Bible Prophecy: Definitive Look at Its Past, Present, and Future* (2d. ed.: Eugene, Ore.: Harvest House, 2005), 280. We should note that Price errs when he differs from most commentators in seeing three questions rather than two.

nation? Especially since he records their witnessing Christ's weeping over Jerusalem (Matt 23:37), hearing him declare the temple desolate (23:38), and joining together in pointing out the beautiful temple buildings (24:1)? This is particularly problematic in that their questions arise from Christ's own statement about the temple's destruction in 24:2, and since they would need to prepare first-century Christians to live through the AD 70 holocaust, which will soon occur.

The proposed gap in Matthew's record cannot credibly stand in such a context. Matthew 24 *must* deal with the destruction of the Temple. In fact, I will show that *all* of the first portion of the Discourse (Matt 24: 4–34) focuses on AD 70. Only after detailing that matter does Christ turn his attention to the world-ending second advent in the latter portion of the Discourse (24:36–25:46).

We begin to surmise this split possibility when we realize the disciples are asking two questions: "Tell us, [1] *when* will these things be, and [2] *what* will be the sign of Your coming, and of the end [*sunteleia*] of the age?" (Matt 24:3). By these "when" and "what" questions they are asking about the *time* of the temple's destruction and the *sign* of his coming which heralds the temple's end — which they (wrongly) associate with the end of the world.[7] In the Greek one definite article governs the last phrase: "*the* sign of your coming and end of the age," thereby showing that this is really only one issue.[8]

The disciples could easily believe that the temple's destruction would herald the end of the world. Hence their linked questions responding to his surprising prophecy. Consider the following evidence in this direction:

(1) Before the outpouring of the Holy Spirit at Pentecost (John 15:26; 16:13; Acts 2:1ff) the disciples are frequently confused about Christ's teaching.[9] For instance, they do not even realize he is going to die and arise again until after these occur (John 20:8–9; cp. 2:22; Matt 28:17). And this is despite his repeatedly teaching them these very things (e.g., Matt

---

[7] Matthew uses the word *sunteleia* (which appears in the phrase "the *end* of the age") only for the world's end: Matt 13:39, 40, 49; 24:3; 28:20.

[8] Though the phrase "the end of the age" could refer to the end of any particular age (depending on context), Matthew seems to reserve it for the end of history (Matt 13:39–40, 49; 28:20). This "age" refers to history as over against the eternal age (12:32).

[9] See: Matt 14:17, 31; 15:15, 33; 16:5–12, 22; 17:10; 18:21; 19:10, 13, 25; 20:24; Acts 11:18.

16:21; 20:18). Also some of them continue to hold Zionistic national expectations (Luke 24:21; Acts 1:6), though he resists such (John 6:15) and defines his ministry in contrary terms (John 18:36–37). (He corrects them on these very issues; Luke 24:25; Acts 1:7.)

(2) The disciples undoubtedly imbibe the Jewish conviction that the temple is a permanent institution (see discussion above, especially the reference from Philo: *Spec. Laws* 1:14 [76]). Thus, for it to be destroyed must signal the end of history.

(3) Theologically, a redemptive-historical link does in fact connect AD 70 with the second advent. This could easily confuse the disciples. That is, the AD 70 episode is an anticipatory foreshadowing of the larger event, the second advent. As Carson expresses it: "The near event, the destruction of Jerusalem, serves as a symbol for the far event," i.e., the second coming."[10] This is akin to there being *several* historical episodes of "the day [singular!] of the Lord" in the Old Testament (Isa 13:6, 9; Eze 13:5; Joel 1:15; 2:1, 11; Amos 5:18, 20; Oba 15; Zeph 1:7; Mal 4:5). Each of these anticipate the final "day of the Lord" event at the end of history (2 Pet 3:10).

"The End"

Before I conclude this chapter I must focus briefly on Jesus' repeated references to the "end." Not only are the disciples confused about the end, but so are modern evangelical Christians who have been swept away with dispensationalism. In our English translations we see the word "end" in five places: Matthew 24:3, 6, 13, 14, and 31. Grasping their actual meaning and their internal narrative linkage will be important for helping us understand the unfolding discourse.

Actually Matthew 24 uses two distinct words for "end": *sunteleia* and *telos*. *Sunteleia* appears only in Matthew 24:3, whereas we find the more common word *telos* in verses 6, 13, 14, and 31.

Despite common assumptions the word *telos* does not necessarily speak of the end of history. In fact, its lexical meaning highlights "the goal toward which a movement is being directed, *end, goal, outcome*" (BAGD 998). That is, it speaks of the conclusion to *any* particular movement, not just the end of *historical development*. We may see this in the following examples of non-eschatological uses:

---

[10] D. A. Carson, "Matthew," in EBC 12:492.

- In Mark 3:26 it points to the end of Satan's kingdom: "If Satan has risen up against himself and is divided, he cannot stand, but he is *finished*!"
- In 2 Corinthians 3:13 it signifies the end of the old covenant order: "and are not as Moses, who used to put a veil over his face that the sons of Israel might not look intently at the *end* of what was fading away."
- Hebrews 7:3 speaks of Christ having no "end of life": "Without father, without mother, without genealogy, having neither beginning of days nor *end* of life, but made like the Son of God, he abides a priest perpetually."
- In James 5:11 it denotes the outcome of God's dealing with Job: "Behold, we count those blessed who endured. You have heard of the endurance of Job and have seen the *outcome* of the Lord's dealings, that the Lord is full of compassion and is merciful."
- Matthew even uses it in a mundane manner in Matthew 26:58 when he speaks of Peter's following after Christ during his arrest so that he can see what the *outcome* will be: "Peter also was following Him at a distance as far as the courtyard of the high priest, and entered in, and sat down with the officers to see the *outcome*."

Matthew appears to distinguish *sunteleia* from *telos* by reserving *sunteleia* as his distinctive term for the eschatological end, the goal of history. In every case where *sunteleia* appears it signifies this eschatological function

- Matthew 13:39–40: "The enemy who sowed them is the devil, and the harvest is the end of the age; and the reapers are angels. Therefore just as the tares are gathered up and burned with fire, so shall it be at the end of the age."
- Matthew 13:49: "So it will be at the end of the age; the angels shall come forth, and take out the wicked from among the righteous."
- Matthew 28:20: "Teaching them to observe all that I commanded you; and lo, I am with you always, even to the end of the age."

Let us quickly survey Matthew's "end" usage in the Olivet Discourse.

As noted, *sunteleia* appears first in Matthew 24:3 and points to the end of history. It appears in the disciples' questions which are packed with their assumption that the world will end when the temple ends: "And as He was sitting on the Mount of Olives, the disciples came to Him privately, saying, 'Tell us, when will these things be, and what will be the sign of Your coming, and of the end of the age?'" (Matt 24:3).

The next appearance of an "end" term is in Matthew 24:6: "And you will be hearing of wars and rumors of wars; see that you are not frightened, for those things must take place, but that is not yet the end." This warns them not to expect the "end" yet. But what end? The end about which they ask. When he states that the temple will be destroyed stone-by-stone (Matt 24:1) they ask: "Tell us when will these things be?" They are referring to the temple. But the signs in verses 5–6 should not "mislead" (v 5) them to think the end of the temple must occur immediately. In fact, in verse 8 he notes that such things are merely "the beginning of birth pangs," not the event itself.

In Matthew 24:13 he encourages them to endure: "but the one who endures to the end, he shall be saved." As France notes, this may indicate either one of two things[11]: (1) It may be urging their faithfulness until the temple is finally destroyed. That is, they must be spiritually strong through all of the upheaval leading to the temple's end. Or it may mean: (2) They must hang on for as long as their struggles take, i.e., to the very end of their trials. That is, they must endure throughout all their persecutional trials, then they will be saved if they do not apostatize. This seems to parallel the sentiment in Matthew 10:22 where he is speaking of persecution rather than the temple's destruction: "you will be hated by all on account of My name, but it is the one who has endured to the end who will be saved."

Then in the very next verse we read: "And this gospel of the kingdom shall be preached in the whole world for a witness to all the nations, and then the end shall come" (Matt 24:14). In this statement Jesus is teaching that the gospel must first go forth to all the world before the temple is finally destroyed (see later discussion). Thus, the "end" here is once again the end of the temple.

Thus, we must understand that Jesus is not applying the Olivet Discourse solely to the end of history. The word *telos* that he repeatedly uses does not require that meaning. When he speaks of the "end" in Matthew 24:6 and 14 he is answering their question about the end of the temple,

---

[11] R. T. France, *The Gospel of Matthew* (NICNT) (Grand Rapids: Eerdmans, 2007), 907.

its destruction. In Matthew 24:13 he is referring neither to the end of the world or the end of the temple, but to the end of their persecution.

Conclusion

Having worked our way through Matthew and covering his abundant preparation for the Olivet Discourse, we are now ready directly to enter into it. Although anyone should be able to understand Christ's teaching here on its own terms, recognizing Matthew's narrative flow is extremely helpful for securing its proper understanding.

Chapter 4
OLIVET'S INTERPRETIVE KEY
Matthew 24:34

Christ's original audience is quite confused initially about his prophecy regarding the soon-coming destruction of the temple (24:2–3). But they should not continue in their confusions when they hear his extended explanation of this remarkable event. After all, despite the strained dispensational interpretation of Matthew 24, the Lord himself expressly states that this will occur in the disciples' own generation. In fact, we discover at least a three-fold witness to this.

The Temporal Indicator

More significant even than Matthew's flow in both its global and local narrative contexts is Christ's statement in Matthew 24:34:

> Truly I say to you, this generation will not pass away until all these things take place.

Here we have a confident, clear, and compelling pronouncement regarding the *time* of the events recorded in 24:4–31. But before we focus on the actual time indicator ("this generation"), we should note how Jesus "solemnly introduced and emphatically affirmed" it.[1] This is no casual statement; he demands that his disciples recognize its significance.

First, Jesus dogmatically asserts its validity. Jesus is emphatic whenever he begins a statement with "truly" (Greek: *amen*). Hendriksen notes of the word: "In every case . . . in which this word occurs in the New Testament it introduces a statement which not only expresses a truth or fact . . . but an *important*, a *solemn* fact, one that in many cases is at variance with popular opinion or expectation or at least causes some surprise."[2] Thus, he emphatically draws the disciples's attention to what he is about to say — just as he does in 24:2, where he makes the initial prophetic announcement regarding the destruction of the Temple that leads to the whole discourse.

---

[1] William Lane, *The Gospel of Mark* (NICNT) (Grand Rapids: Eerdmans, 1974), 479.

[2] William Hendriksen, *Matthew* (NTC) (Grand Rapids: Baker, 1973), 289–90.

Second, Jesus carefully focuses the disciples' attention. He dramatically introduces what he is about to say with the declarative "I say to you." The Lord does not leave the temporal expectation in the background hoping his disciples will catch it. He alerts them to what he is about to say. This is something about which he strongly demands their attention.

Third, Jesus employs a strong negative. The literal rendering of the Greek reads: "Truly I tell you that *by no means* passes away generation this until all these things happen."[3] In Greek the "by no means" translates a strong, double negative: *ou me*. Wallace explains in his authoritative *Greek Grammar Beyond the Basics*: "Emphatic negation is indicated by *ou me* plus the *aorist subjunctive* [as here in Matt 24:34, KLG].... This is the strongest way to negate something in Greek."[4]

Fourth, Jesus places his negation in an emphatic position. He puts *ou me* early in his statement for added emphasis. He is staking his credibility, as it were, on the absolute certainty of this prophetic pronouncement. Indeed, he contrasts the durability and integrity of his prophetic word here with the stability of the material universe: "Heaven and earth will pass away, but My words shall not pass away" (Matt 24:35).

Now we must ask: what does Jesus so dogmatically and deliberately state? He asserts that "*all* these things" he has just prophesied (24:4–31) will occur *before* "this generation" passes away. But what does "this generation" mean?

Alternative Interpretations

Basically there are three leading interpretations of the verse before us. Let us consider them carefully.

"This generation" is "this race"

According to an earlier publication of Pentecost, "the word generation is to be taken in its basic usage of 'race, kindred, family, stock, breed,' so that the Lord is here promising that the nation Israel shall be preserved until the consummation of her program at the second advent

---

[3] Alfred Marshall, *The Interlinear Greek-English New Testament* (Grand Rapids: Zondervan, 1959), 108

[4] Daniel B. Wallace, *Greek Grammar Beyond the Basics: An Exegetical Syntax of the New Testament* ((Grand Rapids: Zondervan, 1996), 468.

The Olivet Discourse Made Easy

. . . . This seems to be the best explanation."[5] Thus, the Lord would be stating that the Jews would not pass away until all these things take place.

This interpretation is without basis for a variety of reasons. First, such a view ends up as a mere truism if "this generation" means "Israel as a nation."[6] For in this reading Christ simply states that Israel will not pass away until all these things happen to Israel. Thus, it ultimately means that Israel will not pass away until Israel passes away. Besides, in the dispensational view "Israel will never pass away"[7] anyway, so the statement would be meaningless on their own interpretive presuppositions.

Second, though the Greek *genea* ("generation") is common in Matthew, *he never* employs it in the sense some dispensationalists call for here. We find it in Matthew 1:17; 11:16; 12:39, 41-42, 45; 16:4; 17:17; and 23:36. Only with great difficulty may an interpreter contort any of these references to mean "Israel as a nation." Such a strained interpretation is a case of special pleading.

Third, in five other instances Matthew couples the word *genea* with the near demonstrative *haute* to read "this generation." In each of these it clearly refers to the generation *then living*. These passages are Matthew 11:16; 12:41, 42, 45; and 23:36. In fact, the immediately preceding reference appears in the historical context of the Olivet Discourse and must mean that first century generation:

> Therefore, behold, I am sending you prophets and wise men and scribes; some of them you will kill and crucify, and some of them you will scourge in your synagogues, and persecute from city to city, that upon you may fall the guilt of all the righteous blood shed on earth, from the blood of righteous Abel to the blood of Zechariah, the son of Berechiah,

---

[5] Pentecost, *Things to Come*, 281 (earlier printing; not later). Cp. L. S. Chafer, *Systematic Theology* (Dallas, Tex.: Dallas Theological Seminary, 1948), 4:316. C. I. Scofield, *Scofield Reference Bible* (New York: Oxford, 1945), 1034. E. Schuyler English, *Studies in the Gospel according to Matthew* (New York, Revell, 1935), 179. William Kelly, *Lectures on the Gospel of Matthew* (New York: Loizeaux, 1911), 451–53.

[6] H. N. Ridderbos, *Commentary on Matthew* (Grand Rapids: Zondervan, 1987), 450.

[7] John F. Walvoord, *Prophecy Knowledge Handbook* (Wheaton: Victor, 1990), 391.

whom you murdered between the temple and the altar. *Truly I say to you, all these things shall come upon this generation*. (Matt 23:34–36)

In Scripture the idea of a "generation" of people involves roughly twenty-five to forty years.[8] Dispensationalist Thomas Ice even admits that "it is true that every other use of 'this generation' in Matthew (11:16; 12:41-42, 44; 23:36) refers to Christ's contemporaries.[9]

"This generation" is "that generation"

In more recent writings Pentecost forsakes his earlier view. He now holds the following position:

> Since these signs will all occur in the seven years of Daniel's seventieth week, the generation that sees the beginning of these signs will "not pass away until all these things happened" (v. 34), for they all will fall within a brief span of time. Notice that these will *not* be signs given to a generation preceding the Rapture. Instead, these signs will be given to a generation that cannot begin until after the church has been translated.[10]

Fellow dispensationalist John F. Walvoord concurs: "The most natural meaning, however, is to take it as normally used as a reference to a period of twenty-five to forty years. But instead of referring this to the time in which Christ lived, it refers back to the preceding period that is described as the great tribulation. As the great tribulation is only three-and-a-half years long, obviously, those who see the Great Tribulation will also see the coming of the Lord."[11] Walvoord refuses to consider the most obvious and legitimate interpretation: that it refers to the generation that actually hears Jesus say this and who witness the destruction of the Temple.

Unfortunately for Pentecost, his new view involves him in question-begging circularity. He considers it obvious that "these signs will be given to a generation that cannot begin until after the church has been translated." Where is the "translation of the church" (i.e., the rapture) in this

---

[8] A. T. Robertson, *Word Pictures in the New Testament*, 6 vols., (Nashville: Broadman, 1930), 1:194. See: Num 32:13; Psa 95:10.

[9] Thomas Ice and Kenneth L. Gentry, Jr., *The Great Tribulation: Past or Future?* (Grand Rapids: Kregel, 1999), 125. See also 103.

[10] Pentecost, *Thy Kingdom Come*, 256. See also: Wiersbe, *The Bible Exposition Commentary*, 1:89. House and Ice, *Dominion Theology*, 286–87

[11] Walvoord, *Prophecy Knowledge Handbook*, 391ff.

passage? As happens too often in dispensational theology, he must *assume* his dispensational system in order to reinterpret the passage to uphold the system. Thus, he holds this as a suppressed premise. In fact, Walvoord notes of Matthew 24: "An important notation should be made at this point that the Rapture of the church and the close of the Church Age is [sic] nowhere mentioned in this prophecy."[12]

And what of Walvoord's statement that "this generation" actually "refers back to the preceding period that is described as the great tribulation"? This also assumes the great tribulation does not occur in the first century — simply because of dispensational requirements. I agree that "this generation" refers to "the preceding period that is described as the Great Tribulation." But then I believe Jesus is clearly speaking to his disciples almost 2000 years ago, when he expressly declares its fulfillment in "this generation." The great tribulation is tied in with the subject of his discourse: the destruction of the Temple (Matt 24:2).

Ice attempts to better secure this view by arguing:

> the governing referent to "this generation" is "all these things." Jesus is giving an extended prophetic discourse of future events, so one must first determine the nature of 'all these things' prophesied in verses 4 through 33 to know what generation Christ is referencing. "All these things" did not take place in the first century, so Christ must be speaking of a future generation. . . . Christ is speaking not to His contemporaries, but to the generation that witnesses the signs of Matthew 24.[13]

But this will simply not work for the following reasons:

First, Ice rather surprisingly states that "Christ is speaking not to His contemporaries"! Yet the whole context shows very clearly that he *is most definitely* speaking to his contemporaries. In fact, he is speaking *only* to his disciples who were his contemporaries:

> And Jesus came out from the temple and was going away when *His disciples* came up to point out the temple buildings to Him. And *He answered and said to them*, "Do *you* not see all these things? Truly I say to *you*, not one stone here shall be left upon another, which will not be torn down. And as He was sitting on the Mount of Olives, *the disciples came to Him privately, saying*." (Matt 24:1–3)

---

[12] Walvoord, *Prophecy Knowledge Handbook*, 381.

[13] Thomas Ice, "Generation, This," in Tim LaHaye and Ed Hindson, eds., *The Popular Encyclopedia of Bible Prophecy* (Eugene, Ore.: Harvest, 2004), 117.

Second, we must remember that his prophecy of the temple's destruction (Matt 24:2) prompts the Olivet Discourse with a view to answering the disciples' question *for them*: "the disciples came to Him privately, saying, 'Tell *us*, when will these things be?" (Matt 24:3). In my fuller analysis of the text, I will show that early in the Discourse he warns them not to become confused by preliminary signs, for "that is not yet the end" (24:6b) and "all these things are merely the beginning of birth pangs" (24:8). So in answering their question regarding "*when* will these things be" he cautions them against being misled by the initial signs This means he is in fact answering their question as to "when these things will be" but has not arrived at the answer yet. It is only at 24:34 that he finally gives them the answer for which they are looking: "Truly I say to you, *this generation* will not *pass away until* all these things take place" (Matt 24:34).

Third, as noted above this statement regarding "this generation" is already defined in the historical context of the Olivet Discourse. In Matthew 23:36 he warns: "Truly I say to you, all these things shall come upon *this generation*." He surely does not expect them to jump from one temporal statement (23:36) to an almost identical one (24:34) in the very same context and require that they interpret the phrases differently. (I will have more to say about this below.)

Fourth, as we reflect on Ice's argument we may easily surmise that he has reversed the actual situation. That is, since Jesus is answering their question regarding "when" these things will be, this temporal statement must govern "these things" rather than vice versa. They were not asking "*what* are 'these thing'"; they are asking "*when* will these things be"?

Fifth, Ice's view requires that Matthew *totally omit* the portion of Christ's answer that touches on the very question the disciples raise. Ice states: "All three Synoptic Gospels (Matthew, Mark, and Luke) record the Olivet discourse as given by Jesus. Matthew and Mark focus exclusively upon the future events of the Tribulation, while Luke's version includes past and future elements."[14] Later he dogmatically claims: "I do not believe that Christ's Olivet discourse contains a single sentence, phrase, or term that *requires* a first-century fulfillment, except for Luke 21:20–24."[15] How can Matthew's reader surmise such? This does not make sense.

Sixth, the material between Matthew 24:4 and the verse in question — v 34 — specifically relates to the judgment on Judea (the region in

---

[14] Thomas Ice in Ice and Gentry, *The Great Tribulation*, 96.

[15] Ice in Ice and Gentry, *The Great Tribulation*, 131.

which Jerusalem is located) and "the holy place" (i.e., the temple 24:16[16]): "Therefore when you see the abomination of desolation which was spoken of through Daniel the prophet, standing in the *holy place* (let the reader understand), then let those who are in *Judea* flee to the mountains" (Matt 24:15–16). Since Jesus has just left the Jerusalem temple (23:38), and the disciples have pointed out the temple buildings (24:1), and he has just pronounced its destruction (24:2), this reference to a "holy place" in "Judea" must be to that very temple. But again, as they are prone to do, dispensationalists create another suppressed premise. In this case the temple Jesus refers to in 24:16 is a future rebuilt temple.

Seventh, Ice's argument is made all the more remarkable when we compare the (supposedly future) great tribulation passage in Matthew 24 with the (past, first century) temple destruction passage in Luke 21. I will place the two texts side-by-side, showing that they are referring to the same event, even though using slightly different language (as the Gospel writers are prone to do):

Matthew 24:15–19	Luke 21:20–23
Therefore when you see the abomination of desolation which was spoken of through Daniel the prophet, standing in the holy place (let the reader understand), then let those who are in Judea flee to the mountains; let him who is on the housetop not go down to get the things out that are in his house; and let him who is in the field not turn back to get his cloak. But woe to those who are with child and to those who nurse babes in those days!	But when you see Jerusalem surrounded by armies, then recognize that her desolation is at hand. Then let those who are in Judea flee to the mountains, and let those who are in the midst of the city depart, and let not those who are in the country enter the city; because these are days of vengeance, in order that all things which are written may be fulfilled. Woe to those who are with child and to those who nurse babes in those days; for there will be great distress upon the land, and wrath to this people.

Ice requires another suppressed premise in the text: an unmentioned rebuilt temple.

---

[16] God's temple is "holy" (1 Chron 29:3; Psa 5:7; 65:4; 138:2), and is "the holy place" in view here.

We find another rather innovative and remarkable dispensational argument regarding "this generation" offered by Randall Price. He argues that when Jesus speaks of "this generation" in Matthew 23:36 he "indicated a *future* generation. It was future from the perspective of the sins 'this generation' (in context) would yet commit (complicity in the crucifixion) and the judgment they would receive (the Roman destruction in A.D. 70)." He then argues regarding "this generation" in Matthew 24:34: "If the desolation experienced by 'this generation' in Matthew 23:36 can be understood as a future fulfillment that came some 40 years later, it should not be a problem to understand the Tribulation judgment of the Olivet Discourse as having a future fulfillment that will come upon the generation that will experience it at the end of the age."[17]

Price's argument fails on two considerations. First, he is arguing that if "this generation" can speak of a generation forty years in the future, surely it can stretch to 2000+ years. That is not very persuasive. Second, the biblical concept of a "generation" is generally deemed to be around forty years. This happens to cover the whole generation from when Jesus speaks (AD 30) to the destruction of the temple (AD 70).[18]

The Correct Interpretation

Having seen dispensationalist efforts to foist their system upon the Olivet Discourse, let us now consider the proper interpretation of Christ's "this generation" statement.

Actually a simple reading of Matthew 24:34 leads to the inescapable conclusion that "these things" are to occur in the first-century generation of Christ's original audience. Thus, we may say (as strange as it may seem) that "this generation means this generation." Though Ice laments that 24:34 "has been one of the most controversial passages in Bible prophecy,"[19] contextual exegesis helps us resolve the (alleged) "problem" regarding its meaning. The phrase "this generation" appears in the very context intimately related to and ultimately introducing Matthew 24.

---

[17] Randall Price, *The Temple and Bible Prophecy: A Definitive Look at Its Past, Present, and Future* (2d. ed.: Eugene, Ore.: Harvest, 2005), 279.

[18] See: Num 32:13; Psa 95:10.

[19] Thomas Ice, "Generation, This," in LaHaye and Hinson, *Popular Encyclopedia of Bible Prophecy*, 116.

In Matthew 23:36 "this generation" unquestionably speaks of Jesus's contemporaries, as even most dispensationalists admit.[20] Here Jesus is condemning his adversaries, the scribes and Pharisees (Matt 23:2, 13, 14, 16, 23, 25, 26, 27, 29). He specifically observes that his opponents will "fill up the measure of the guilt" of their predecessors (23:32). They will do this by persecuting his followers (23:34), so that "upon you [scribes and Pharisees] may fall the guilt of all the righteous blood shed" (23:35). He concludes: "Truly I say to you, all these things shall come upon this generation" (23:36).

Now we should note some of the identical phrases in Matthew 23:36 and 24:34, which show they must be speaking of the same generation:

Matthew 23:36	Matthew 24:34
Truly I say to you	Truly I say to you
all these things	this generation
this generation	all these things

Because of such observations, D. A. Carson speaks of the "highly artificial" attempts by dispensationalists to reinterpret the word "generation." He argues that it is obvious the word "can only with the greatest difficulty be made to mean anything other than the generation living when Jesus spoke."[21] Dispensationalist David Turner agrees:

> Although some futurists argue that the word refers either to the nation of Israel or to the eschatological generation that is alive at Jesus's coming . . , the use of the term clearly shows that Jesus is talking about his contemporaries.[22]

Matthew's constant use of the phrase "this generation" ties us directly to the first century. To drive home the point I will list each of the other occurrences of the phrase in Matthew (excluding Matt 24:34 which is the one I am analyzing).

---

[20] Barbieri, "Matthew," in Edward E. Hinson and Woodrow Michael Kroll, *Liberty Commentary on the New Testament* (Lynchburg, Vir.: Liberty Commentary, 1978), 75. John F. Walvoord, *The Nations, Israel, and the Church in Prophecy*, 3 vols. in 1 (Grand Rapids: Zondervan, 1988), 2:106. Pentecost, *Thy Kingdom Come*, 249. Ice in Ice and Gentry, *The Great Tribulation*, 103–04.

[21] D. A. Carson, "Matthew" in EBC, 8:507.

[22] David L. Turner, *Matthew* (BECNT) (Grand Rapids: Baker Academic, 2008), 586.

> Matthew 11:16
> But to what shall I compare *this generation*? It is like children sitting in the market places, who call out to the other children.

Here Jesus is speaking to his contemporaries who are witnesses to his coming. He notes that that generation rejects both his forerunner John the Baptist (Matt 11:18) and him (11:19). Immediately after this statement Matthew writes: "Then He began to reproach the cities in which most of His miracles were done, because they did not repent" (11:20).

> Matthew 12:41–42
> The men of Nineveh shall stand up with *this generation* at the judgment, and shall condemn it because they repented at the preaching of Jonah; and behold, something greater than Jonah is here. The Queen of the South shall rise up with *this generation* at the judgment and shall condemn it, because she came from the ends of the earth to hear the wisdom of Solomon; and behold, something greater than Solomon is here.

Here Jesus denounces those rejecting him much like he does in Matthew 11. He notes that Gentiles will stand as witnesses against those who are rejecting his teaching. Nineveh repented at Jonah's preaching, but now Jesus' generation is rejecting him: "something greater than Jonah is here" (Matt 12:41). He notes that the Queen of the South went to hear Solomon's wisdom, but that Israel is currently rejecting Jesus' teaching despite the fact that "something greater than Solomon is here" (12:42).

> Matthew 23:36
> Truly I say to you, all these things shall come upon this generation.

As noted above he utters this judgment statement because of the current scribes and Pharisees who will persecute his followers (Matt 23:2, 29, 34). This leads him to weep over Jerusalem (23:37) and declare desolate her temple in which he is standing (23:38, cp. 24:1).

Thus, Jesus is expressly teaching that his preceding prophetic declarations in Matthew 24:4–31 — "all these things" (Matt 24:34) — will occur in "this generation." And just forty years later the Jewish War with Rome brings the total and final destruction of the Temple (24:2). I agree with premillennial Puritan scholar John Gill: "This is a full and clear proof, that not any thing that is said before [v. 34], relates to the second coming of Christ, the day of judgment, and the end of the world; but that all belong to the coming of the son of man, in the destruction of Jerusalem, and to the end of the Jewish state."[23]

Significantly we should note that Jesus also prefixes "truly" and " I say to you" (Matt 24:34) to three other prominent imminence statements embedded in Matthew's record. And in each of these he is clearly speaking of the first-century generation:

> But whenever they persecute you in this city, flee to the next; for truly I say to you, you shall not finish going through the cities of Israel, until the Son of Man comes. (Matt 10:23)

Here we have two indications that he is referring to the first century: (1) He speaks of the persecution of his followers, which is the main thrust of his denunciation of the scribes and Pharisees in first-century Jerusalem (Matt 23:34–37), as well as the record we find in Acts (e.g., Acts 8:1; 9:1–4[24]). (2) He ties this judgment-coming of the Son of Man to his disciples' ministry to Israel, informing them that they will not finish their mission to Israel before that judgment comes. Surely he is not referring to an event hundreds upon hundreds of years away.

> Truly I say to you, there are some of those who are standing here who shall not taste death until they see the Son of Man coming in His kingdom. (Matt 16:28)

Here once again we have two evidences that he is speaking of the first century expectation that the Son of Man will come in his kingdom, which must mean in AD 70: (1) He is speaking of "some" of those "who are standing here." Not all, but certainly some. (2) These "some" will "not taste death until" they witness this glorious event.

> Truly I say to you, all these things shall come upon this generation. (Matt 23:36)

In this statement the Lord once again prefaces his declaration with "truly I say to you." And in this case he is speaking of the first-century scribes and Pharisees (Matt 24:2, 34) while lamenting first-century Jerusalem's

---

[23] John Gill, *An Exposition of the New Testament*, 9 vols., (Streamwood, Ill.: Primitive Baptist Library, rep. 1976), 7:296.

[24] See also: Acts 4:1–3, 15–18; 5:17–18, 27–33, 40; 6:12–15; 7:54–60; 13, 21, 23, 29; 12:1–3; 13:45–50; 14:2–5, 19; 17:5–8, 13; 18:6, 12, 17; 20:3, 19; 21:11, 27–32; 22:3–5, 22–23; 23:12, 20–21; 24:5–9, 27; 25:2–15; 25:24; 26:21; 28: 17–29. Compare: Rom 15:31; 1 Cor 15:9; 2 Cor 11:24; Gal 1:13; 6:12; Phil 3:6; 1 Tim 1:12–13; Heb 10:33–34.

spiritual rejection of him during his early ministry (23:37). No other era witnessed his coming and his rejection; only "this generation" in which he ministered.

Before engaging the actual Discourse verse-by-verse, I will introduce the major literary witness to the temple's destruction in AD 70: Flavius Josephus.

Our Historical Witness

Flavius Josephus is a non-Christian, Palestinian Jew, who is an historian of priestly descent. He lives from about AD 37 to 101, overlapping virtually the entire apostolic era.

The Jews begin their revolt against Rome in the summer of AD 66. By November the Syrian legate Cestius Gallus leads the Roman Twelfth Legion against Jerusalem to put down the revolt. For some unknown reason he suddenly retreats from Jerusalem, is chased by the Jews, and his army is almost totally destroyed. The Jews interpret this as a miracle showing God's blessings upon them, thereby inflaming the Jewish sentiment for war to escape bondage to Rome.

When the full-scale Jewish War against Rome breaks out in earnest in AD 67,[25] Josephus initially serves as a general in the Jewish forces. During the War he suffers defeat by the Romans at Jotapata, surrendering to the Roman general Flavius Vespasian. He befriends Vespasian by interpreting a prophetic oracle to mean that Vespasian would one day be emperor of Rome.[26] He then works with Vespasian attempting to get his fellow-Jews to surrender, hoping they will cease their hopeless cause.

Tragically, the Jews do not listen to his entreaties and carry on their fateful war against Rome. During the three and one-half year war (Spring AD 67 — August AD 70). Emperor Nero dies (June AD 68), igniting the Roman Civil Wars. This ultimately results in Vespasian becoming emperor in AD 69.

After the war Josephus returns to Rome with Vespasian and becomes a Roman citizen. Because of his help during the Jewish War, he also becomes a client of Vespasian. He changes his name from the very Jewish Joseph Ben Matthias to a more Roman Flavius Josephus, taking on his benefactor's name.

---

[25] See my *Before Jerusalem Fell: Dating the Book of Revelation* (3d ed.: Fountain Inn, S.C.: Victorious Hope, 2010 [rep. 1997]), ch. 14.

[26] Suetonius, *Vespasian* 6.

Vespasian sponsors Josephus' writing of several important history books. His most famous book *The Wars of the Jews* details the Jewish War, the fall of Jerusalem, and the destruction of the temple. Josephus produces this work about AD 75, just five years after Jerusalem's fall.

In this work Josephus writes as an eyewitness historian who happens to be in the action on both sides of the conflict. His work is extremely valuable, providing indispensable insights into many of the events of the War. I will be citing it frequently, following the example of the early church father, Eusebius (AD 263–339) who did so as he explained the Olivet Discourse (*Eccl Hist* 3:5). Eusebius introduces his account with these words:

> But the number of calamities which everywhere fell upon the nation at that time; the extreme misfortunes to which the inhabitants of Judea were especially subjected, the thousands of men, as well as women and children, that perished by the sword, by famine, and by other forms of death innumerable, — all these things, as well as the many great sieges which were carried on against the cities of Judea, and the excessive. sufferings endured by those that fled to Jerusalem itself, as to a city of perfect safety, and finally the general course of the whole war, as well as its particular occurrences in detail, and how at last the abomination of desolation, proclaimed by the prophets, stood in the very temple of God, so celebrated of old, the temple which was now awaiting its total and final destruction by fire, — all these things any one that wishes may find accurately described in the history written by Josephus. (*Eccl. Hist.* 3:5:4)

At *Ecclesiastical History* 3:7:1 Eusebius states: "It is fitting to add to these accounts the true prediction of our Saviour in which he foretold these very events."

Conclusion

I have covered a lot of material in four whole chapters and have yet to enter into a exposition of the Olivet Discourse. Though the reader may be chomping at the bit to get into the discourse proper, my first four chapters are necessary preparation for making Jesus' famous Discourse understandable. This has been important in that the name of this book is *The Olivet Discourse Made Easy*.

Thus, before actually engaging the Olivet Discourse I have presented some vitally important interpretive information. In chapter one I show that the discourse does not occur out of the blue, clear sky. Indeed, the whole drift of Matthew prepares us for this tragic prophecy of Israel's judgment leading to the temple's destruction. Matthew's whole story contains fore-rumblings of the thunderclap contained in Matthew 24.

In chapter two I narrow this wider context of Matthew to consider the immediately preceding *impetus* to Olivet which we find in Matthew 23. Matthew carefully sets up the final preparation for the Lord's Discourse with a focus on the first-century scribes and Pharisees who will prompt the first persecution of the fledgling church which Jesus establishes.

In chapter three I noted the focus of the entire Olivet Discourse. I showed that Matthew 24:2 expressly declares the destruction of the temple and verse 3 highlights the spark igniting the fiery discourse: the disciples' questions to Christ regarding when these things shall be and what will be their sign.

In the present chapter I turned our attention to the key for properly interpreting the discourse. That key is Jesus' statement in Matthew 24:34 which dogmatically and emphatically declares: "Truly I say to you, this generation will not pass away until all these things take place."

It is only now after all of this preparation that we may enter into a discussion of the particulars of the Olivet Discourse. We are now fully prepared to see what Jesus is teaching his disciples — and us.

I will be adapting an outline for the AD 70 portion of the Discourse which France suggests in his NICNT commentary on Matthew:

I. That Is Not Yet the End (Matt 24:4–14)
II. The Beginning of the End (Matt 24:15–28)
III. The End (Matt 24:29–31)

Chapter 5
FALSE EXPECTATIONS OF THE END
Matthew 24:4–14

Having carefully introduced the Olivet Discourse's in Matthew's narrative setting, we are finally — *and only now!* — ready to engage the text itself. I will open with an appropriate plea to the reader, which is taken from R. T. France's large technical commentary on Matthew:

> At this point I would simply urge the reader to refrain from prejudging the issue simply because this exegesis conflicts with the traditional [i.e., the currently dominant American dispensational — KLG] interpretation, and to try to hear Jesus' words as they would have been heard by his Jewish disciples as they listened to this answer to their double questions, as yet uninfluenced by a tradition which conditions Christian readers now to assume that 'the stars falling from heaven' and 'the Son of Man coming on the clouds of heaven' *can only* refer to the end of the world and the *parousia*.[1]

So let us begin!

As we engage the opening of the actual discourse, we must recall that the disciples specifically ask Jesus about the *time* of the temple's stone-by-stone destruction (Matt 24:2): "Tell us, *when* will these things be" (24:3a). Thus, Matthew's record of the actual discourse begins with the words: "Jesus answered and said to them" (24:4a). They ask "when", and Jesus begins answering them. And again, they associate this with the end [*suneteleia*], i.e., of the world (24:3b). Since they ask "when," they show a concern for the timing of the event.

Given the disciples' tendency to confuse matters, the Lord opens with an appropriate warning: "See to it that no man misleads you" (Matt 24:4b). France notes that he is here offering "pastoral guidance for puzzled disciples in unsettling times."[2] This is terribly important in that Jesus will soon establish the Lord's Supper, remind them he will be dying, and will state: "You will all fall away because of Me this night, for it is written,

---

[1] R. T. France, *The Gospel of Matthew* (NICNT) (Grand Rapids: Eerdmans, 2007), 893.
[2] France, *Matthew* (NICNT), 901.

'I will strike down the shepherd, and the sheep of the flock shall be scattered'" (26:31). He is warning them against false-starts.

False Christs (Matt 24:5)

In Matthew 24:5 Jesus specifically warns: "for many will come in My name, saying, 'I am the Christ,' and will mislead many." This is a particularly significant problem in the first century because many Jews are fervently anticipating a conquering political Messiah (which is one reason they reject Jesus).[3] Thus, we even read of some of Jesus' over zealous listeners who try "to come and take Him by force, to make Him king" (John 6:15) and Pilate's concerned judicial inquiry: "Are You the King of the Jews?" (John 18:37a). We should remember their short-lived enthusiasm as he enters Jerusalem for the last time: In Matthew 21:9 their cry "Son of David" betrays their nationalistic expectations. Their soon rejecting him while preferring Barabbas shows their disappointment (Matt 27:20). We clearly see their commitment to a political revolutionary as Messiah just sixty years after the AD 70 destruction of the temple. Under the emperor Hadrian in AD 132 Bar Kochba set himself up as the Messiah and revolted against Rome, only to be destroyed along with Jerusalem. Even the famous Jewish sage Rabbi Akhibah endorsed his Messiahship stating "a star has shot off Jacob" (referring to the Messianic prophecy in Num 24:17).

This first-century expectation is largely due to the famous prophecy in Daniel 9. Gaston notes that "Dn 9 is the only passage in the whole Old Testament to give any possibility of predicting the time of the end."[4] Evangelical scholar F. F. Bruce agrees.[5] As Josephus himself comments regarding Daniel's prophecies: "he did not only prophesy of future events, as did the other prophets, but he also determined the time of their accomplishment" (*Ant* 10:11:7 [267]). Jesus is warning his disciples not to be caught up in such a Zionistic frenzy for he is the Christ who was to come.

---

[3] Matt. 2:1–18; Luke 24:21; John 1:20, 41; 4:29; 7:27, 31; 11:47–48; 12:34. See also the Jewish apocalyptic literature surrounding the New Testament era: The Psalms of Solomon; 4 Ezra; Apocalypse of Baruch; the Dead Sea Scrolls (1QSb 5:20; 4Q Patriarchal Blessings).

[4] Lloyd Gaston, *No Stone On Another: Studies in the Significance of the Fall of Jerusalem in the Synoptic Gospels* (Leden: Brill, 1970), 461.

[5] F. F. Bruce, *Josephus and Daniel* (Leiden: Brill, 1965).

Jewish theologian Abba Hillel Silver had done extensive research in ancient Jewish messianic expectation. In this research he reports of the era in which Jesus prophesies:

> The first century, however, especially the generation before the destruction [of the temple], witnessed a remarkable outburst of Messianic emotionalism. This is to be attributed, as we shall see, not to an intensification of Roman persecution but to the prevalent belief induced *by the popular chronology of that day* that the age was on the threshold of the millennium.[6]

Heniz Schreckenberg (an internationally reputed scholar of Jewish history and an associate at the Institutum Delitzchianum of Judaica in Münster) has written[7]:

> It is first necessary to view briefly the 'messianic scenario' of the post-Herodian period before 70, and above all the persons, groups and movements mentioned by Josephus that can more or less be characterized as 'messianic':[8]
>
> 1. Justus son of Ezekias (*Ant.* 17:271–72 [17:10:5]; *War* 2:[4:1] 56).
> 2. Simon of Peraea (*Ant.* 17:273–276 [17:10:6]; *War* 2:57–59 [2:4:1]
> 3. A movement similar to the group led by Simon of Peraea (*Ant.* 17:277 [17:10:5]; *War* 2:59 [2:4:1]).
> 4. Athronges (*Ant.* 17:278–85 [17:10:6]; *War* 2:60–65 [2:4:1]).
> 5. Judas of Galilee (*Ant.* 18:4–9 [18:1:1], 23–25 [18:1:6]; *War* 2:117–118 [2:8:1]).
> 6. Theudas (*Ant.* 20:97–98 [20:5:1]).
> 7. The Egyptian false prophet (*Ant.* 20:169–172 [20:8:6]; *War* 2:261 –263 [2:13:5]).
> 8. The 'impostor' (*goes*; *Ant.* 20:188 [20:8:10]).
> 9. The religious enthusiasts who led their followers into the wilderness (*Ant.* 20:167–168 [20:8:6]; *War* 2:258–260 [2:13:4]).
> 10. Manaemos (Menahem), son of Judas of Galilee (*War* 2: 433–440 [2:17:7]).

---

[6] Abba Hillel Silver, *A History of Messianic Speculation in Israel: From the First through the Seventeenth Centuries* (New York: Macmillan, 1927), 5.

[7] Guthrie, *New Testament Introduction*, 21.

[8] France (*Matthew* [NICNT], 902) suggests a reason Josephus avoids all references to "Christ" in his record of the Jewish War. It is because the term has political overtones and since he was now a patron of Rome after the costly Jewish War he wisely avoided use of this charged term. Thus, we should not discount all his Messianic-like references simply because they do not actually use the term.

11. Simon bar Giora (*War* 4:514–544, 556ff, 563ff [4:9:5–8, 10], and elsewhere).
12. John of Gischala (*War* 4:389ff [4:7:1] and elsewhere).
13. The Samaritan Messiah (*Ant.* 18:85–87 [18:4:1]).
14. Jonathan the Weaver (*War* 7:437–450 [7:7:1]; *Life* 242–425 [47]). His activities took place in the period ca. 71–73, after the fall of Jerusalem in 70, but by their nature are connected to the period 66–70.
15. Rome-hating imposters' (*goets*; *War* 2:264–265 [2:13:6]).
16. A false prophet in Jerusalem who prophesied God's salvation even after the burning of the Temple (*War* 6:285 [6:5:2]).

I will quote of few of Josephus' comments by way of illustration. Regarding Judas the Galilean who misleads "a great part of the people" Josephus notes:

> Now it came to pass, while Fadus was procurator of Judea, that a certain magician, whose name was Theudas, persuaded a great part of the people to take their effects with them, and follow him to the river Jordan; for he told them he was a prophet, and that he would, by his own command, divide the river, and afford them an easy passage over it; and many were deluded by his words. (*Ant* 20:5:1 [97–98])

Regarding many deceivers and the Egyptian prophet we read:

> And now these impostors and deceivers persuaded the multitude to follow them into the wilderness, and pretended that they would exhibit manifest wonders and signs, that should be performed by the providence of God. And many that were prevailed on by them suffered the punishments of their folly; for Felix brought them back, and then punished them. Moreover, there came out of Egypt about this time to Jerusalem one that said he was a prophet, and advised the multitude of the common people to go along with him to the Mount of Olives, as it was called, which lay over against the city, and at the distance of five furlongs. He said further, that he would show them from hence how, at his command, the walls of Jerusalem would fall down; and he promised them that he would procure them an entrance into the city through those walls, when they were fallen down. (*Ant* 20:8:6 [167–70])

Thus, we have records of many pretenders who "will mislead many" (Matt 24:5b) and who almost certainly make Messianic claims. Some deceivers even appear in the biblical record. Not long after Christ's ascension we read of Simon Magus who may be an example of such. He was "astonishing the people of Samaria, claiming to someone great; and they all, from smallest to greatest, were giving attention to him, saying, 'This man is what is called the Great Power of God'" (Acts 8:9–10). Justin Martyr (AD 100–65) speaks of Simon Magus and others: "after Christ's ascension into heaven the devils put forward certain men who said that they themselves were gods."[9] Hippolytus (AD 160–236) records that "there arose some, saying I am Christ, as Simon Magus, and the rest whose names I have not time to reckon up."[10]

John mentions such false Christs in his first epistle, where he calls them "antichrists": "Little children, it is the last hour; and as you have heard that the Antichrist is coming, even now many antichrists have come, by which we know that it is the last hour" (1 John 2:18). As Robertson notes of 1 John 2:18: "So Jesus taught (Mark 13:6, 22; Matt. 24:5, 15, 24) and so Paul taught (Acts 20:30; 2 Thess. 2:3). These false Christs . . . are necessarily antichrists, for there can be only one. *Anti* can mean substitution or opposition, but both ideas are identical in the word *antichristos*."[11]

As noted above by Schreckenberg such characters play an important role in the religious, social, cultural, and political foment that leads to the AD 67–70 Jewish War with Rome. The great church historian Philip Schaff comments that Israel of that era "rose to the most insolent political and religious fanaticism, and was continually inflamed by false prophets and Messiahs, one of whom, for example, according to Josephus, drew after him thirty thousand men."[12] Divine irony allows those who reject the true Christ to be frequently and devastatingly duped by false Christs.

Abba Hillel Silver, a key Jewish promoter of the founding of the state of Israel in 1948, writes: "The first century, however, especially the generation before the destruction [of the temple], witnessed a remarkable outburst of Messianic emotionalism. This is to be attributed, as we shall see, not to an intensification of Roman persecution but to the prevalent belief induced *by the popular chronology of that day* that the age was on the threshold of the millennium."[13] He argues that Josephus mentions Messi-

---

[9] Martyr, *First Apology* 26.

[10] *The Consummation of the World*.

[11] A. T. Robertson, *Word Pictures in the New Testament* (Nashville: Broadman, 1930), 6:215. Dispensationalists agree: Paul N. Benware, *Understanding End Times Prophecy: A Comprehensive Approach* (Chicago: Moody, 1995), 249.

[12] Philip Schaff, *A History of the Christian Church* (3rd. ed.: Grand Rapids: Eerdmans, 1910), 1:394.

[13] Abba Hillel Silver, *A History of Messianic Speculation in Israel: From the First through the Seventeenth Centuries* (New York: Macmillan, 1927), 5

anic calculation which he applied to Vespasian (*J.W.* 6:5:4 [312–13]). Josephus' statement is as follows:

> But now, what did the most elevate them in undertaking this war, was an ambiguous oracle that was also found in their sacred writings, how, "about that time, one from their country should become governor of the habitable earth." The Jews took this prediction to belong to themselves in particular, and many of the wise men were thereby deceived in their determination. Now this oracle certainly denoted the government of Vespasian.

Wars and Rumors of Wars (Matt 24:6–7a)

One of the signs so often mentioned in the current discussion appears in Matthew 24:6–7a: "And you will be hearing of wars and rumors of wars; see that you are not frightened, for those things must take place, but that is not yet the end. For nation will rise against nation, and kingdom against kingdom."

How can wars be a useful sign? As Cambridge scholar and classical historian Michael Grant has noted war has been "raging almost continuously throughout the centuries."[14] Dispensationalist Wiersbe seeks to side-step this problem by commenting: "Note that wars are not a sign of the end. There have always been wars in the world, and will be until the very end. Wars of themselves do not announce the end of the age nor the coming of the Lord."[15]

It is true, of course, that "wars of themselves" do not announce the immediate end. But because of dispensationalism's large investment in futurism, they fail to interpret this passage contextually.

This passage, however, is quite relevant to the situation of Jesus's hearers, his disciples (Matt 24:2–3) of "this generation" (24:34). As usual, a little familiarity with the cultural and political situation existing in that era is most helpful. "Wars and rumors of wars" do serve as *sign*-ificant harbingers of the end — *of the Temple,* which is the major issue being discussed (Matt 23:38–24:3). This sign is relevant and significant because of the dramatically successful *pax Romana*, the "peace of Rome."

---

[14] Michael Grant, *The Ancient Historians* (New York: Charles Scribners, 1970), 27.

[15] Warren W. Wiersbe, *Bible Exposition Commentary* (Wheaton, Ill.: Victor, 1989), 2:87.

The *pax Romana* begins with Augustus's establishment of the "Age of Peace" in 17 BC. He is able to effect this wide-spread, long-lasting peace by creating the Roman imperial army which "was the earliest of the world's standing armies in which the soldiers were regularly recruited, and cared for, and finally pensioned off, by the state" and became "one of the greatest and most formidable armies that has ever existed."[16] It is an imposed peace, to be sure, but a remarkable peace nevertheless.

Roman naturalist Pliny the Elder (AD 23–79) describes "the immeasurable majesty of the Roman peace."[17] Greek Stoic philosopher Epictetus (AD 55–135) writes that "Caesar has obtained for us a profound peace. There are neither wars nor battles" (*Discourses* 3:13:9). Christian theologian Origen (AD 185–254) comments about the "abundance of peace that began at the birth of Christ" (Origen, *Romans* 1:3).

Famed Church historian Eusebius (AD 260–340) also refers to this remarkable time: "What slanderous lip shall dare to question that universal peace to which we have already referred, established by his power throughout the world? For thus the mutual concord and harmony of all nations coincided in point ot time with the extension of our Saviour's doctrine and preaching in all the world" (*Oration* 17:12). He also states that "profound peace reigned throughout the world" (*Oration* 16:4).

Thus, the first century is indeed a time of an "abundance of peace" that gives stability to the Mediterranean basin and, by the providence of God, allows for the rapid dissemination of the Christian faith.

Interestingly, scholars observe that "in the Roman Empire proper, this period of peace remained comparatively undisturbed *until the time of Nero.*"[18] Nero (lived: AD 37–68; ruled AD 54–68) is the emperor who formally engages the Jewish War that results in the destruction of the Temple stone-by-stone. In his Olivet Discourse, the Lord is giving signs for the temple's destruction (Matt 24:2–3). These signs really begin to erupt in a world-shaking manner when Nero dies in the midst of the Jewish War (June AD 68).

At Nero's death the *pax Romana* is severely breached. At that time the Roman Civil Wars erupt, including the turbulent "Year of Four Emperors"

---

[16] Michael Grant, *The Army of the Caesars* (New York: Charles Scribner's, 1974), xv.

[17] Cited in Grant, *Army of the Caesars*, xv.

[18] Bo Reicke, *The New Testament Era: The World of the Bible from 500 BC to AD 100* (Philadelphia: Fortress, 1968), 110.

(June AD 68 — June 69). In fact, the turmoil of this period is so severe that it almost leads to the collapse of the Roman Empire.[19] Consequently, as the events begin unfolding up to the Jewish War, the Christians remember Christ's prophecy of the coming devastation of Jerusalem, which will be the great tribulation (as we shall see).

Thus, the "wars and rumors of wars" are truly signs for that "generation." The outbreak of wars in such an era would serve as an impressive, unexpected, and unimaginable sign in an era of such remarkable peace imposed by such an enormously powerful empire. Josephus marvels at Rome's world dominance: He calls the Romans "the lords of the habitable earth" (*J.W.* 4:3:10 [178]; cp. *Ant* 19:1:2 [14]) and Rome "the greatest of all cities" (*J.W.* 4:11:5 [656]). Regarding the Jews "they must know that the Roman power was invincible [*ischu anupostaton*]" (*J.W.* 5:9:3 [365]) so that "the universe is subject to Rome [*upocheiria ta panta*]" (*J.W.* 5:9:3 [366]). Indeed, "the power of the Romans is invincible in all parts of the habitable earth" and to them "all the world hath submitted" (*J.W.* 2:16:4 [361, 362]). "Almost every nation under the sun does homage to the Roman arms" (*J.W.* 2:16:4 [380]). "In the habitable world all are Romans" (*J.W.* 2:16:4 [388]) for "they are now lords of the habitable earth" (*Apion* 2:4 [4]).[20]

What is more, Rome's engagement with Israel in the Jewish War involves the imperial army with contributions of troops and horsemen from Rome's client kings and allies. Josephus mentions soldiers from Caesarea, Syria, Arabia, and other cities and nations. (*J.W.* 3:1:3–4 [6–34]). Significantly, Josephus entitles his most famous work of the era "The Wars of the Jews."

Furthermore, during the Roman Civil Wars (AD 68–69) several nations revolt in an attempt to leave the Empire. Tacitus mentions the Gallic provinces, Britain, Germany, Sarmatae, and Suebi.[21] It literally is a time of "nation against nation."

Thus, whereas Jesus' day is a time of great peace known as the *pax Romana*, he warns that wars and rumors of wars will disrupt it. The dis-

---

[19] Josephus notes of the Roman Civil Wars of this era: "I have omitted to give an exact account of them, because they are well known by all, and they are described by a great number of Greek and Roman authors" (*J.W.* 4:9:2 [492]). For more information see my *Before Jerusalem Fell*, 311–314.

[20] See also *J.W.* 2:1:13 [354]; 2:16:4 [353]; 4:3:10 [178].

[21] Tacitus, *Hist* 1:2–3.

ruptive wars occur in Nero Caesar's latter days and lead to the destruction of Jerusalem and the Temple. Nevertheless, the disciples must not be "frightened" because "those things must [*dei*] take place." The word *dei* speaks of divine necessity: God is in control.

They must also understand that these disruptive wars do not signal the *immediate* end: "but that is not yet the end" (Matt 24:6c). Here the Greek word used for "end" is *telos* rather than *sunteleia* (as at 24:3). As I noted previously, the word *telos* carries the connotation of "the goal toward which a movement is being directed, *end, goal, outcome*" (BAGD 998). Jesus is not yet referring to the end of history, but in this specific context he is speaking of the end of the temple which he prophesies earlier (24:2; cp. John 4:21; Heb 8:13).

Famines (Matt 24:7b)

Christ continues preliminary signs by warning that "in various places there will be famines and earthquakes" (Matt 24:7b). We may also see these occurring in the first century.

Acts 11:28 mentions a devastating, empire-wide famine in the days preceding Nero's reign, in the reign of Claudius (reigned: AD 41–54): "And one of them named Agabus stood up and began to indicate by the Spirit that there would certainly be a great famine all over the world. And this took place in the reign of Claudius." This is probably the famine Josephus mentions as striking Jerusalem: "A famine did oppress them at that time, and many people died for want of what was necessary to procure food withal" (*Ant* 20:2:5 [51]; cp. 20:2:3 [37]).

There is also the well-known famine that rages in Jerusalem during the Roman siege. Josephus reports the following:

> the madness of the rebellious did also increase together with their famine, and both those miseries were every day inflamed more and more; for there was no corn which any where appeared publicly, but the robbers came running into, and searched men's private houses; and then, if they found any, they tormented them. (*J.W.* 5:10:2 [424])

> But the famine was too hard for all other passions, and it is destructive to nothing so much as to modesty; for what was otherwise worthy of reverence was in this case despised; insomuch that children pulled the very morsels that their fathers were eating out of their very mouths, and what was still more to be pitied, so did the mothers do as to their infants; and when those that were most dear were perishing under their hands, they were not ashamed to take from them the very last drops that might preserve their lives. (*J.W.* 5:10:3 [429–30])

There was a certain woman that dwelt beyond Jordan, her name was Mary. . . . it was now become impossible for her any way to find any more food, while the famine pierced through her very bowels and marrow, when also her passion was fired to a degree beyond the famine itself; nor did she consult with any thing but with her passion and the necessity she was in. She then attempted a most unnatural thing; and snatching up her son, who was a child sucking at her breast, she said, "O thou miserable infant! for whom shall I preserve thee in this war, this famine, and this sedition? As to the war with the Romans, if they preserve our lives, we must be slaves. This famine also will destroy us, even before that slavery comes upon us. Yet are these seditious rogues more terrible than both the other. Come on; be thou my food, and be thou a fury to these seditious varlets, and a by-word to the world, which is all that is now wanting to complete the calamities of us Jews." As soon as she had said this, she slew her son, and then roasted him, and eat the one half of him, and kept the other half by her concealed. Upon this the seditious came in presently, and smelling the horrid scent of this food, they threatened her that they would cut her throat immediately if she did not show them what food she had gotten ready. She replied that she had saved a very fine portion of it for them, and withal uncovered what was left of her son. Hereupon they were seized with a horror and amazement of mind, and stood astonished at the sight, when she said to them, "This is mine own son, and what hath been done was mine own doing! Come, eat of this food; for I have eaten of it myself! Do not you pretend to be either more tender than a woman, or more compassionate than a mother; but if you be so scrupulous, and do abominate this my sacrifice, as I have eaten the one half, let the rest be reserved for me also." After which those men went out trembling, being never so much affrighted at any thing as they were at this, and with some difficulty they left the rest of that meat to the mother. Upon which the whole city was full of this horrid action immediately; and while every body laid this miserable case before their own eyes, they trembled, as if this unheard of action had been done by themselves. So those that were thus distressed by the famine were very desirous to die, and those already dead were esteemed happy, because they had not lived long enough either to hear or to see such miseries. (J.W. 63:3:4 [201, 204–13])

For a mother to eat her own child is a sign of covenant curse (Deut 28:55–57; Lam 2:20), which Israel endures for rejecting their Messiah (Matt 27:25). Jesus weeps over Jerusalem with these words: your enemies "will level you to the ground and your children within you, and they will not leave in you one stone upon another, because you did not recognize the time of your visitation" (Luke 19:44).

Classical writers testify to the widespread, recurring famines of the era of the AD 50s through the 60s, as we discover in the works of Suetonius, Dio Cassius, Eusebius, and Orosius.[22] For instance, of AD 51 the Roman historian Tacitus writes: "This year witnessed many prodigies.... Further portents were seen in a shortage of corn, resulting in famine.... It was established that there was no more than fifteen days' supply of food in the city [Rome]" (*Ann* 12:43).

Earthquakes (Matt 24:7c)

The Lord also mentions earthquakes along with the famines in Matthew 24:7b: "in various places there will be famines and earthquakes."

Philostratus (AD 172–250) writes the *Life of Apollinius* (who died in AD 75). He mentions earthquakes during this time in Smyrna, Miletus, Chios, Samos and several of the Iades.[23] He reports a particularly large quake which occurred while Apollonius was prophesying in Crete:

> An earthquake shook the whole of Crete at once, and a roar of thunder was heard to issue not from the clouds but from the earth, and the sea receded about seven stadia. And most of them were afraid that the sea by receding in this way would drag the temple after it, so that they would be carried away.... After a few days some travelers arrived from Cydoniatis and announced that on the very day on which this portent occurred and just at the same hour of midday, an island rose out of the sea in firth between Thera and Crete."[24]

Tacitus mentions earthquakes in Crete, Rome, Apamea, Phrygia, Campania, Laodicea (of Revelation fame) and Pompeii during the time just before Jerusalem's destruction.[25] Severe earthquakes plague the reigns of the Emperors Caligula (AD 37–41) and Claudius (AD 41–54).[26] According to Seneca (*ca.* 4 BC—AD 65), others occur in Asia, Achaia, Syria, and Macedonia.[27] Of this era, Ellicott's commentary observes: "Perhaps no

---

[22] See: Suetonius, *Life of Claudius* 18:2; Dio Cassius, *History* 60:11; Eusebius, *Chronicle*, Year of Abraham 2065; Orosius, *History* 7:6:17.

[23] Flavius Philostratus, *Life of Apollinius*, 4:6.

[24] Philostratus, *Apollonius*, 4:34.

[25] See Roman historians: Tacitus, *Ann* 2:47; 12:58 14:27; 15:22; Pliny, *Nat Hist* 2:86; and Suetonius, *Nero* 48; *Galba* 18. See also: Philostratus, *Life of Apollion*, 4:11 and Orosius 7:7.

[26] W. J. Coneybeare and J. S. Howson, *The Life and Epistles of St. Paul*, 2 vols., (New York: Charles Scribner's, 1894), 1:126.

[27] Seneca, *Epistles* 91.

period in the world's history has ever been so marked by these convulsions as that which intervenes between the Crucifixion and the destruction of Jerusalem."[28]

But more important for the disciples who originally hear Jesus' discourse are quakes in the region of Jerusalem itself, the epicenter of the great tribulation. A particularly dreadful quake shakes Jerusalem in AD 67 as the Jewish War is breaking out. Josephus records this frightful catastrophe:

> There broke out a prodigious storm in the night, with the utmost violence, and very strong winds, with the largest showers of rain, and continual lightnings, terrible thunderings, and amazing concussions and bellowings of the earth, that was in an earthquake. These things were a manifest indication that some destruction was coming upon men, when the system of the world was put into this disorder; and any one would guess that these wonders foreshowed some grand calamities that were coming. (J.W. 4:4:5 [286–87])

Birth Pangs (Matt 24:8)

As these portents appear on the historical scene, the disciples must be aware that these are but "the beginning of birth pangs." This is quite suggestive. This term speaks of acute suffering and has no specific referent and is not reserved for final-eschatological events. The Old Testament uses this imagery for God's wrath befalling men in history (Isa 13:8; Jer 6:24; 22:23; Mic 4:9–10[29]). The rabbis frequently use this word as a technical Messianic term in the phrase "birth pangs of the Messiah."[30] The rabbinic phrase refers to the distress that will precede the Messianic era.

Jesus employs the term "birth pangs," then, to point to a new *beginning* even as the Temple era approaches a dismal end. He uses the birth pang imagery in John 16:21 as he informs his disciples he will soon be leaving this world. He noted that though birth pangs bring sorrow, they presage joy at a birth. For the disciples these troubles in Matthew 24 are the birth pangs of the kingdom. *Because of these birth pangs, the future is*

---

[28] Charles John Ellicott, ed., *Ellicott's Commentary on the Whole Bible*, (Grand Rapids: Zondervan, n.d.), 6:146.

[29] See also: Isa 26:17; 66:7–8; Jer 4:31; 22:23; 30:5–6; 48:41; Hos 13:13; Mic 5:3.

[30] See: b. *Ketuboth* 111a; b. *Shabbath* 118a; b. *Sanhedrin* 98b; Targum on Psa 18:4; Targum on 2 Sam 22:5.

bright with hope, even if sore with the pain of labor. As Jerusalem goes up in smoke, Christ's kingdom enters into its own life, separating from its "mother" (Israel).

As he tells them earlier: "Verily I say unto you that there be some of them that stand here, which shall not taste of death, till they have seen the kingdom of God come with power" (Mark 9:1). This event lay sufficiently in the future that some hearing him would die before it becomes evident "with power." Yet it is close enough that others would live to witness it. This cannot be a reference to the Transfiguration which occurs only six days later (9:2). How many of them will die before that event? The same holds true for the outpouring of the Spirit at Pentecost (Acts 2). It must be the AD 70 destruction of the temple, occurring forty years later.

The salvation Christ secures will make victorious headway in the world, expanding the spiritual principle of the new creation (2 Cor 5:17; Eph 2:10; 6:17). As the old Jerusalem and temple era end, the New Jerusalem (Gal 4:23–31; Rev 21:1–2; cp. Rev 22:6, 10[31]) and new temple (Eph 2:20–21; 1 Pet 2:5) begin in earnest. The Epistle to the Hebrews speaks of the approaching demise of the old covenant temple order and the firm establishment of the new in its place. In Hebrews 8:13 we read: "When He said, 'A new covenant,' He has made the first obsolete. But whatever is becoming obsolete and growing old is ready to disappear" (Heb 12:18–28; cp. John 4:21). Then shortly thereafter we read further regarding the presence of "the heavenly Jerusalem" (Heb 12:22), the removing of the old covenant temple system so that the new covenant kingdom may remain in it place (Heb 12:27–28).

In fact, the New Testament looks with holy anticipation to the final change from the old order to the new order, as the Temple system approaches its dramatic disestablishment in AD 70. A major redemptive transformation takes place in the apostolic era between AD 30 and AD 70. This transition leads to "the restoration of all things" (Matt 17:11), "the regeneration" (Matt 19:28), the "times of refreshing" (Acts 3:19), the "times of the restitution of all things" (Acts 3:21), the "time of reformation" (Heb 9:10), a "new heavens and a new earth" (Rev 21:1; cp. 2 Cor 5:17; Gal 6:17), "all things new" (Rev 21:5 [cf. 22:6, 10]; cp. 2 Cor 5:17; Gal 6:15).

---

[31] See my: "The Preterist View," in C. Marvin Pate, ed., *Four Views on the Book of Revelation* (Grand Rapids: Zondervan, 1998).

Thus, the temple's destruction dramatically confirms the coming of the new covenant era that Christ legally inaugurates. Since Christ's first-century coming, we have been living in the "last days" (Acts 2:17; 1 Cor 10:11; Heb 1:2; 9:26; 1 Pet 1:20; 1 John 2:18). The last days begin in earnest in the transitional era between Christ's death and the temple's destruction; they stretch from the first coming to his second coming, ending with the "last day" at the resurrection (John 6:39–44; 11:24). There are no other days to follow — no 365,000 days (i.e., 1000 years) of Christ's reign upon the earth will succeed these "last days." The former days — old covenant Israel's times — have expired. These are now the *last* days.[32]

Persecution and Apostasy (Matt 24:9–10)

In Matthew 24:9 the Lord warns his disciples that they must expect *persecution*: "Then they will deliver you up to tribulation and kill you, and you will be hated by all nations for My name's sake." We may easily demonstrate the fulfillment of this prophecy by Jewish opposition in Acts.[33] This summarizes Matthew 10:17–21 and continues Christ's warning in Matthew 23:34–36 — and clearly applies to the first century. After the initial *Jewish* persecution of Christians comes hatred "by all nations," i.e., the first Roman imperial onslaught just preceding the temple's destruction (AD 64–68).[34] The pagan Roman historian Tacitus speaks of Christians in the era of Nero as universally "hated for their crimes."[35]

We discover a sad consequence of this severe persecution in Matthew 24:10: "And at that time many will fall away and will deliver up one another and hate one another." That is, many who have professed Christ will "fall away" and will even "deliver up one another and hate one ano-

---

[32] For more information on this optimistic view of history, see: Kenneth L. Gentry, Jr., *Postmillennialism Made Easy* (Draper, Vir.: ApologeticsGroup Media, 2010).

[33] See for example: Acts 4:3; 5:18-33; 6:12; 7:54–60; 8:1ff; 9:1–4, 13, 23; 11:19; 12:1-3; 13:45–50; 14:2-5, 19; 16:23; 17:5-13; 18:12; 20:3, 19; 21:11, 27; 22:30; 23:12, 20, 27, 30; 24:5–9; 25:2–15; 25:24; 26:21. See also: 2 Cor 11:24; 2 Thess 2:14-15; Heb 10:32–34; Rev 2:9; 3:9.

[34] The Neronic persecution is the first and most grievous Roman persecution. It stretches from around November, AD 64 to the death of Nero, June 8, AD 68. See discussion in my *Before Jerusalem Fell*, ch. 5.

[35] Tacitus, *Ann* 15:44.

ther." We may document this, too, in the biblical record of the apostolic era. Paul laments "that all who are in Asia turned way from me" (2 Tim 1:15) and "Demas, having loved this present world, has deserted me" (2 Tim 4:10). He comments that "at my first defense no one supported me, but all deserted me" (2 Tim 4:16; cp. Gal 3:1–4; 2 Thess 3:1).

The Apostle John writes of apostasy in the first century: "They *went out from us*, but they were not of us; for if they had been of us, they would have continued with us; but they went out that they might be made manifest, that none of them were of us" (1 John 2:19; cp. 2 and 3 John). The Epistle to the Hebrews indicates a sizeable apostasy from among Jewish converts to Christianity (cf. Heb. 2:1–4; 6:1–6; 10:26–31). Tacitus alludes to apostasy during the Neronic persecution just before the Jewish War: "First, Nero had self-acknowledged Christians arrested. Then, *on their information*, large numbers of others were condemned."[36]

False Prophets and Lawlessness (Matt 24:11–13)

"False prophets" also become a problem in the first century. "Now when they had gone through the island to Paphos, they found a certain sorcerer, a false prophet, a Jew whose name was Bar-Jesus" (Acts 13:6). Peter, Paul, and John all warn about this danger.[37]

Josephus also records false prophets arising among the Jews — and in such a way as to be a danger to any who would listen to them:

> A false prophet was the occasion of these people's destruction, who had made a public proclamation in the city that very day, that God commanded them to get upon the temple, and that there they should receive miraculous signs of their deliverance. Now there was then a great number of false prophets suborned by the tyrants to impose on the people, who denounced this to them, that they should wait for deliverance from God; and this was in order to keep them from deserting, and that they might be buoyed up above fear and care by such hopes. Now a man that is in adversity does easily comply with such promises; for when such a seducer makes him believe that he shall be delivered from those miseries which oppress him, then it is that the patient is full of hopes of such his deliverance (*J.W.* 6:5:2 [285–87]).

---

[36]Tacitus, *Ann* 15.
[37]See also: Acts 20:29; Rom 16:17,18; 2 Cor 11:13, 26; 1 Tim 4:1; 2 Pet 2:1; 1 John 4:1. Cp. Gal 2:4; 2 Pet 2:1.

These false prophets in Jerusalem during the war aggravate the destruction of the city by buoying up the hopes of the zealots.

Regarding these sad circumstances Jesus declares: "because lawlessness is increased, most people's love will grow cold" (24:12). Persecution, betrayal, and apostasy signify a state of lawlessness arising within the Christian community.[38] This "lawlessness" is breaching of God's Law which includes turning against true Christians (Matt 22:39–40; Gal 5:14) and defecting from one's professed faith (Num 14:11–12; Deut 13:1–4). Within the first-century church this lawlessness causes the love of many to grow cold. Jesus is speaking here of the love expected of Christians for one another. He teaches that the mark of a true disciple is love for one another (John 13:34–35; 15:12, 17). The rest of the New Testament emphasizes this truth (Rom 13:8; 1 Thess 4:9; 1 Pet 1:22; 1 John 3:11, 13, 23; 4:7, 11–12, 20). Tragically that defining love will fade as professed believers "fall away" and "deliver up one another and hate one another" (24:10).

The idea involved in "fall away" does not reflect a temporary stumbling and momentary spiritual setback. Rather the Lord is speaking of an absolutely destructive collapse of faith resulting in apostasy. The word for "fall away" here is *skandalizomai*. It appears in other contexts in Matthew where it clearly speaks of absolute rejection of the truth from those who initially accept the truth (Matt 5:29–30; 13:21; 18:6–9).

Because of all of this, Jesus urges his disciples to endure these troublesome times: "the one who endures to the end, he shall be saved" (Matt 24:13). Here he reiterates what he taught earlier in Matthew 10:22: "You will be hated by all on account of My name, but it is the one who has endured to the end who will be saved." The chaos leading up to and surrounding the Temple's destruction ("the end" in view) will eventually cease. Those who maintain faith in Jesus and endure the terrible struggles will be saved — not only physically through the dangerous upheaval that finally ceases, but (most importantly) *spiritually* as they cling to their faith.

---

[38] I formerly held that this "lawlessness" was referring to the wicked conditions prevailing in Jerusalem when it was under siege (as reported by Josephus). See: my *Perilous Times: A Study in Eschatological Evil* (Texarkana, Ark.: CMF, 1999, 52–53). However, a closer reading of the context suggests Jesus is still speaking of the apostasy/betrayal problem that will affect his church in the first century even before the Jewish War with Rome.

The Gospel in the Whole World (Matt 24:14)

Many discount the argument for the fulfillment of the general precursory signs in Matthew 24:4–13 as adaptable to any era of history since the days after Christ. And they most certainly are — but only if abstracted from their context. But at verse 14 some argue that the preterist position is impossible because of the teaching here. Matthew 24:14 reads:

> And this gospel of the kingdom shall be preached in the whole world for a witness to all the nations, and then the end shall come.

How can we possibly argue that the gospel was preached in the "whole world" before AD 70 and the temple's destruction? This is made all the more difficult in that its presentation must be "to all the nations"!

The preterist problem

Of Matthew 24:14 dispensationalists Wayne House and Thomas Ice write:

> If we look closely at Matthew 24:14 we notice that there are two phrases which modify "shall be preached" — "in the whole world" and "to all the nations." In the first phrase, the adjective "whole" indicates that it is the world in its totality that is in view.[39]

They then parallel the next phrase to that of Matthew 28:19, arguing for a universal proclamation of the gospel to "all the nations" literally. They challenge the preterist by asking: Are you "saying that the gospel was preached before AD 70 in the Western hemisphere?"[40]

The *PEBP* entry titled "Olivet Discourse" agrees:

> Matthew 24:14 describes a future event and parallels Revelation 14:6–7. Both passages are set in contexts that tell us that this global evangelization will take place just before the middle of the seven-year Tribulation. They were no more fulfilled during the nativity of the church than was the Great Commission. Matthew 24:14, like all of those prophecies in that context, awaits a future fulfillment — specifically, during the future Tribulation.[41]

The more scholarly commentary on Matthew in the Baker Exegetical Commentary also accepts this interpretation. While discussing Matthew 24:14 David Turner writes:

---

[39] House and Ice, *Dominion Theology*, 298.
[40] House and Ice, *Dominion Theology*, 298.
[41] *PEBP*, 253.

> This perseverance will result in the kingdom message... being preached to all the nations before the end comes (cf. 10:22–23; 28:18–20)....
> Matthew 24:4–14 summarizes the difficulties the church will face in the early days before 70 CE and throughout its existence.[42]

But this futurist analysis is not as strong as it initially seems. Once again, we must keep in mind Jesus' temporal indicator ("this generation," Matt 24:34), his original audience (the disciples who ask when the Temple would be destroyed, Matt 24:2–3), and the harmony of the preceding signs with the first century experience. Actually, when carefully considered the text before us does not state what futurists believe it does. Note the following responses that we may make against the futurist analysis:

(1) The meaning of the term. The word "world" here is the Greek word *oikoumene*, which occurs only here in Matthew. It very often means the Roman Empire, as we can see in the following sample passages from the New Testament:

> And it came to pass in those days that a decree went out from Caesar Augustus that all the world should be registered. (Luke 2:1, NKJV)

> Then one of them, named Agabus, stood up and showed by the Spirit that there was going to be a great famine throughout all the world, which also happened in the days of Claudius Caesar. (Acts 11:28)

Can anyone argue that the Roman emperor was attempting to register residents in "the Western Hemisphere," as per House and Ice's query? Note that the text clearly states that this registration was designed for "all the world."

And do we really believe that the famine during Claudius' reign actually reached across the Atlantic Ocean into "the Western Hemisphere"? Here in Acts 11 we even find the same key words as in Matthew 24:14: *holos* ("whole") + *oikumene* ("world").

(2) The supplementary information. What does he mean by the additional phrase that supplements "in the whole world"? That phrase reads: "to all the nations."

In adding these words Jesus is emphasizing an important point. He is doubling the focus of the gospel proclamation: it is to be both to "the whole world" and to "all the nations." This is significant in that it shows he is removing his earlier restriction upon his disciples where he limited

---

[42] David L. Turner, *Matthew* (BECNT) (Grand Rapids: Baker, 2008), 574–75.

their ministry to the borders of Israel (the Land) and to the Jews (the people) alone (Matt 10:5; 15:24). But here he is prophesying that his message will eventually go out into the broader world beyond the borders of Israel. This becomes clear in his Great Commission at the end of his earthly ministry when he finally initiates the full-scale Gentile ministry (Matt 28:18–20).[43]

We should understand also that the word for "nations" is *ethnos*. This word indicates "a body of persons united by kinship, culture, and common traditions" and "people groups foreign to a specific people group" (BAGD 276). Thus, *ethnos* could even be translated (as it often is in the New Testament) "Gentiles." It is a term that distinguishes other people groups from the Jews. In fact, *ethnos* is the very word that appears in Jesus' earlier ministry limitation: "These twelve Jesus sent out after instructing them, saying, 'Do not go in the way of the *Gentiles*, and do not enter any city of the Samaritans'" (Matt 10:5).

Interestingly, even as he limits their earlier ministry to Israel he anticipates a future broader testimony among the "Gentiles" (*ethnos*), i.e., the non-Jews: "you shall even be brought before governors and kings for My sake, as a *testimony to them and to the Gentiles*" (Matt 10:18).

So then, by this additional phrase in Matthew 24:14 he is simply saying: My gospel shall be preached to people groups beyond the Jews before "the end [*telos*]" (of the temple) occurs.

The preterist explanation

Now let me point out the fulfillment of the Matthew 24:14 prophecy in the first century. Can we claim that "the gospel of the kingdom" was "preached in the whole world"? Indeed, we can — and on the basis of the biblical record itself.

In Acts 2:5 Luke records the composition of the crowd hearing Peter's pentecostal sermon: "Now there were dwelling in Jerusalem Jews, devout men, from *every nation under heaven*." Using House and Ice's approach we could dispute Luke's record: surely there were no representatives from the "Western Hemisphere," were there? Yet Luke records that men are there "from every nation under heaven" — and the Western Hemisphere

---

[43] As I note in my first chapter this outreach to the Gentiles is hinted at earlier in the Gospel. For instance, in Matt 2 the Gentile Magi come to worship the newborn Christ. In Matt 8:11–12 Jesus teaches that the Gentiles will come and worship with Abraham, Isaac, and Jacob.

is certainly "under heaven." Obviously Luke does not mean to include the Western Hemisphere; to press his words in that direction would be patently wrong.

Here in Acts 2:5, then, we have a gathering to hear the witness of the gospel. This gathering meets the requirements of Matthew 24:14, at least *representationally*, for these people were "from every nation under heaven." But there is more.

In Romans 10:18 Paul states regarding gospel preachers: "Their sound has gone out to all the earth, and their words to the ends of the world [*oikoumenes*]." Thus, Paul can state in AD 55 that "the word of Christ" (Rom 10:17) has *already* gone [aorist verb: past tense] "to the ends of the *oikumene*. Was he stating that these words had penetrated to the Western Hemisphere?

Interestingly, in Romans 1:8 Paul writes: "First, I thank my God through Jesus Christ for you all, that your faith is spoken of throughout the whole world." Their faith is the Christian faith, and Paul dogmatically states that it is being spoken of throughout the "whole world." What is remarkable about this statement is that Paul uses a term for "world" that generally applies more broadly than *oikoumene*.

Here Paul uses the word *kosmos* that often means the entire planet, "the sum total of everything here and now, *the world, the (orderly) universe*" (BAGD 561). This word appears in texts that even mention the creation of the world at the beginning (Matt 13:35; 25:34; Luke 11:40; John 17:5; Rom 1:20; Heb 4:3; 9:26) — and even in our very context in Matthew 24, at verse 21. If Paul can state that the faith of these Christians is being spoken of throughout "the whole world" (*holo to kosmo*) around AD 55, does not this fulfill Jesus statement in Matthew 24:14?

Elsewhere Paul also speaks of the gospel "which has come to you, just as in all the world [*kosmo*]. . . . [T]he gospel that you have heard, which was proclaimed [aorist participle: past] in all creation under heaven" (Col 1:6, 23). Turner discounts these references on the basis that Paul still longs "to take the gospel to previously unreached regions (Spain)."[44] But the point remains: if Paul can state Romans 10:18 and Colossians 1:6 and 23 as *fact* in his lifetime, why may we not see these as *fulfillments* of Matthew 24:14?

---

[44] Turner, *Matthew*, 575.

Before moving on, I would note a couple of other samples of such global assertions used in a limited context. Josephus can speak of Nebuchadnezzar's concern regarding those that would succeed him "in the government of the whole world" (*tou kosmou pantos*) (*Ant* 10:10:4 [205]). And Eusebius traces the history of the early church under the apostles, noting that Christ's message "ran through the whole world" (*panta ton kosmon*) (*Eccl. Hist.* 2: "Contents" III).

Matthew 24:14 is no hindrance at all to the preteristic viewpoint. In fact, it harmonizes beautifully with many other Scriptures — much more easily than does dispensationalism's view that must run roughshod over the clear statement of Matthew 24:34.

This statement is significant as Jesus declares the coming destruction of the temple. Earlier he speaks of himself as greater than Israel's temple (Matt 12:6). He is thus setting himself up as the greater new temple into which he must gather his new people. When we get to Matthew 24:31 we will see the worldwide gathering that begins in earnest with the temple's AD 70 destruction. France observes that "the end of the old order will be the cue for the establishment of the universal reign of the Son of Man and the gathering of a new people of God from the ends of the earth."[45]

Conclusion

This survey of Jesus' opening statements should confirm that he is speaking of first-century events that his first followers will have to endure. We have seen that not only does all of Matthew's earlier chapters anticipate God's judgment upon Israel, not only does the immediately preceding chapter expressly declare God's judgment upon Israel, not only does Jesus give the Olivet Discourse in response to the disciples' question regarding his prophecy that it will be destroyed, and not only does Jesus expressly declare that the events prior to Matthew 24:34 shall come upon "this generation," but now his opening salvo provides historically-verifiable expectations that confirm all of this.

Now as we move further into the discourse we will come upon two types of statements that confuse many: (1) statements that do not appear to apply to the first century; and (2) statements that appear to be impossible for the first century. I will begin dealing with these in the next chapter.

---

[45] France, *Matthew* (NICNT), 911.

Chapter 6
The Beginning of the End
Matthew 24:15–28

In this chapter I will begin entering into the very heart of the Olivet Discourse. All the necessary preliminary studies are out of the way; at verse 15 the Lord begins building toward a crescendo. And as his Discourse does so we will discover verses that appear more difficult to assimilate into the preterist approach. I will show, however, that even these statements that sound as if they are prophesying events lying in our future easily apply to the first-century events.

Prior to this point Jesus clearly taught that "the end is not yet" (Matt 24:6). Now we are moving into the section that actually introduces the beginning of the end. In Matthew 24:14, the immediately preceding verse, Jesus states that the gospel must be preached to all nations "and then the end shall come." The next verse is chronologically significant in that it declares: "*therefore* when you see...." Thus, he is now moving into a presentation of the beginning of the end that he is now ready declare (hence, "therefore"). He will begin dealing with issues directly related to the siege of Jerusalem (Matt 24:15–28).

So let us now consider:

The Abomination of Desolation

We come now to the most famous and least understood portion of the Olivet Discourse — the abomination of desolation passage (Matt 24: 15–28). The dispensationalist holds that this entire episode "is still future."[1] Indeed, while discussing Matthew 24:15–26, Walvoord comments: "One of the sources of confusion among interpreters of the Olivet Discourse is their attempt to find complete fulfillment of the entire Olivet Discourse in connection with the destruction of Jerusalem."[2] We will see,

---

[1] John F. Walvoord, *Prophecy Knowledge Handbook* (Wheaton, Ill.: Victor, 1990), 387.

[2] I agree that it is an error to discover the fulfillment of the *entire* Olivet Discourse in AD 70. I do firmly believe, though, that the events up through v 33 have found such fulfillment (cf. Matt. 24:34). See discussion below.

though, that this is not a source of "confusion" at all for the preterist interpretation — in fact, it exposes confusion in the dispensational system.

Demonstrating the tenuous nature of the dispensational approach to prophecy, I would point out that while dealing with the abomination of desolation Walvoord offers a table of the "Predicted Order of Prophetic Events Related to Israel." These events are supposed to lead up to and/or surround that prophetically significant time.[3] What are some of these "predicted" and "prophetic" events allegedly revealed in Scripture? I will list just two samples from Walvoord's table:

2. United Nations recognizes Israel as a nation and allows 5,000 square miles of territory.
4. The United States becomes her principal benefactor and supplier of military aid and money.

Unfortunately, he neglects to provide us with the biblical passages relating to the United Nations, its formal approval of nationhood for Israel, the 5,000 square miles of territory, the United States, and so forth. Contrary to Walvoord's concern, those who do not find the United Nations and the United States in Bible prophecy are not confused at all. Nor are they impressed by his table, including even progressive dispensationalists who bemoan such.[4]

The meaning of "abomination"

The key statement in this whole passage is Matthew 24:15 which reads:

> Therefore when you see the abomination of desolation which was spoken of through Daniel the prophet, standing in the holy place (let the reader understand).

This horror leads Jesus to warn:

> then let those who are in Judea flee to the mountains; let him who is on the housetop not go down to get the things out that are in his house; and let him who is in the field not turn back to get his cloak. But woe to those who are with child and to those who nurse babes in those days!

---

[3] Walvoord, *Prophecy Knowledge Handbook*, 382–83.
[4] "This type of dispensationalism also popularized apocalyptic readings of the Bible in terms of current history." Darrell L. Bock, "Charting Dispensationalism," *Christianity Today*, 38 (September 12, 1993), 26–28.

But pray that your flight may not be in the winter, or on a Sabbath (Matt 24:16–20)

The first question we must ask is: What does Jesus mean by "the abomination of desolation"? The meaning of this phrase certainly does not jump out at us today. In fact, Carson notes that even among commentators this phrase is " hard to understand."[5] What does it signify?

To properly understand this phrase we must keep in mind that the Lord is speaking to his first-century, Jewish disciples (Matt 24:1, 3) who live in the context of the Old Testament Scriptures and within the old covenant economy. In the Old Testament an "abomination" especially relates to the desecration of worship, either by outright false worship (Deut 7:25; 27:15) or by the profaning of true worship (Lev 7:18; Deut 17:1).

Here in Matthew 24:15 we must note that this "abomination of desolation" occurs in "the holy place," i.e., the temple and/or Jerusalem. Despite Walvoord and other dispensationalists, we may apply this passage to Israel's holocaust in AD 70. This phrase refers to a "'spiritually loathsome' defilement and destruction."[6] Actually, due to Matthew 24:34 the burden of proof is on the dispensationalist to prove their case for a *future* interpretation of this event. The more natural reading of the text is the preterist view. This is so for several reasons:

(1) As Jesus utters these prophetic words a temple is standing in a "holy city" (as Matthew notes, Jerusalem is the holy city, Matt 4:5; 27:53). Jesus' audience and Matthew's readers could imagine no other referent. To suppose a future *rebuilt* temple here (as per dispensationalism) *must be proved*, not assumed.

(2) Christ speaks these words in response to the disciples's observations on that specific temple in Jerusalem of their own day: "His disciples came to Him *to show* Him the buildings of *the Temple*" (Matt 24:1). Indeed, their inquiry sparks his entire discourse (Matt 23:38–24:3).

(3) Christ points to that very temple standing before them in the holy city of Jerusalem: "see ye not all these things" (Matt 24:2), i.e., "the temple buildings" (Matt 24:1[7]). He then speaks of the destruction of those

---

[5] D. A. Carson in *The Expositor's Bible Commentary*, ed. Frank E. Gaebelein (Grand Rapids: Zondervan/Regency, 1981), 12:489.

[6] Gibbs, *Jerusalem and Parousia*, 184.

[7] Mark's rendering of their question highlights the "wonderful stones" in addition to the "wonderful buildings" (Mark 13:1). The stones are what he prophesies will be thrown down (Matt 24:2; Mark 13:2).

buildings: "not one stone shall be left on another that shall not be thrown down" (Matt 24:2). This certainly involves "desolation" and, as I will show, includes *abominable* acts. Thus, we may reasonably surmise that the "abomination of desolation" involves this first-century temple.

Interestingly, when speaking of Jerusalem's destruction, Josephus uses the word *eremothe* ("desolation"): "And thus was Jerusalem taken, in the second year of the reign of Vespasian, on the eighth day of the month Gorpeius [Elul]. It had been taken five times before, though this was the second time of its *desolation*" (*J.W.* 6:10:1 [435]). This is the verbal form of the noun "desolation" (*eremoseos*) that Christ uses in Matthew 24:15.

Furthermore, Josephus, like Christ, also applies Daniel's prophecy to this event: "In the very same manner Daniel also wrote concerning the Roman government, and that our country should be made desolate [*eremothesetai* from *eremothe*] by them" (*Ant* 10:11:7 [276]). Jesus expressly states: "when you see the abomination of desolation spoken of through Daniel the prophet" (Matt 24:15).

(4) And of course, Jesus' clearly declared time-frame demands an AD 70 reference for the "abomination": "Assuredly, I say to you, this generation will by no means pass away till *all* these things are fulfilled" (Matt 24:34).

To assist in interpreting this difficult verse we can turn to the account as recorded by Luke in Luke 21:21. Luke is a Gentile[8] who interprets the wording found in Matthew's very Jewish account. Thus as often happens, Luke uses language that the Gentile might more easily understand. Rather than employing the obscure Old Testament phrase "abomination of desolation" (from Dan 9:27 as recorded in Matt 24:15), he writes: "But when you see Jerusalem *surrounded by armies, then know that its desolation is near*" (Luke 21:20).

Unfortunately, the intricate, pre-conceived, anti-contextual system of dispensationalism confuses evangelicals today. But if we merely lay the passages side-by-side we should be able quickly to convince the casual reader that the *same* events are in view. And this is despite dispensationalists making a radical distinction between Luke 21:20 and Matthew

---

[8] The name *Loukas* is Greek, not Hebrew. In Col 4:11, 14 Paul distinguishes Luke's name from those of the "circumcision," i.e., the Jews. In Acts 1:19 Luke speaks of the Jews' language as "*their* proper tongue." These indicate he is a non-Jew.

24:15: they hold that Luke's statement points to the AD 70 event and that Matthew's speaks of an event in our future.[9]

Matt 24:15–18	Luke 21:20–21
Therefore when you see the *abomination of desolation* which was spoken of through Daniel the prophet, standing in the holy place (let the reader understand), then let those who are in Judea flee to the mountains; let him who is on the housetop not go down to get the things out that are in his house; and let him who is in the field not turn back to get his cloak.	But when you see Jerusalem surrounded by armies, then recognize that her *desolation* is at hand. Then let those who are in Judea flee to the mountains, and let those who are in the midst of the city depart, and let not those who are in the country enter the city.

The holy place

The "abomination of desolation" is so dreadful people will flee desperately from the area. This horrible action will occur "in the holy place." The reference to "the holy place" might seem to speak only of the temple itself and nothing more. Surely the temple is involved, *but the reference is broader, speaking of both the city and the temple*. Several problems present themselves to the narrow temple-only view:

(1) Luke clearly interprets the phrase as the surrounding of the city "Jerusalem" (Luke 21:21). And Jerusalem itself is a holy place,[10] being the capital of the "holy land" (Zech 2:12).[11]

(2) The prophecy calls for flight from all of Judea (the region surrounding Jerusalem), not just the Temple environs. This is why Christ weeps over *Jerusalem* just before uttering this prophecy (Matt 23:37). Christ is warning of *Jerusalem's* devastating destruction, not just the temple's desecration by profane actions. The rising storm of war, not the corrupting spread of heresy, prompts flight from the region.

(3) The original Old Testament context to which Jesus refers mentions both "the city and the sanctuary" (Dan 9:26). Daniel 9:25 even calls Jeru-

---

[9] See: Walvoord, *Prophecy Knowledge Handbook*, 386; J. Dwight Pentecost, *Thy Kingdom Come* (Wheaton: Victor, 1990), 249.

[10] Neh. 11:1, 18; Isa. 48:2; 52:1; 66:20; Dan. 9:16, 24; Joel 3:17.

[11] For Jewish references to Israel as the "holy land," see: 2 Baruch 63:10; 4 Ezra 13:48; 2 Maccabees 1:7.

salem "the holy city" (whereas Matthew speaks of "the holy place"). In fact, the original prophecy pivots on the rebuilding of the *city* (Dan 9:25).[12]

To limit the reference solely to the temple is surely unwarranted. The preceding context of Matthew agrees with Daniel in involving *both* the *city* and the *temple* (Matt 23:37–38). Indeed, the reason Jerusalem is a "holy city" is because in her is God's "holy temple" (1 Chron 29:3; Psa 5:7; 65:4; 138:2; Jon 2:4). I would point out that Josephus speaks often of the "holy house" (*J.W.* 1:18:3 [354]); 1:21:1 [402]; 4:5:4; 5:1:5; etc.; the "holy temple" (*J.W.* Pref. 4 [10]; 2:8:5 [129]; 7:8:7 [379]; etc.; and the "holy city" (*J.W.* 2:16:4 [397]; 4:4:3 [241]; 7:8:7 [379]); etc.

The Judean context

This abomination during the great tribulation focuses on the temple and Jerusalem, not the entire world. Note the following: (1) The event focuses on "they holy place" (Matt 24:15), which is in Jerusalem. (2) Jesus warns the disciples to "flee" (24:16). If this were a worldwide event flight would not help. (3) He warns only "those who are in Judea" to flee (24:16). (4) He holds forth the hope that flight from the area would spare them (24:17–20), again indicating its local nature. This leads us to note the historical record of what occurs in Judea. Therefore we must consider:

Josephus on Jerusalem's destruction

The phrase "the abomination of desolation" summarily designates the events leading up to the destruction of Jerusalem and the temple by the Roman armies. The holy city where the Jews worship God in his holy temple will suffer abominable acts resulting in utter desolation. Josephus gives us a clear record of this occurring in the first century, especially after the surrounding of Jerusalem.[13]

---

[12] For a full exposition of Dan 9:24–27 see Kenneth L. Gentry, Jr., *Perilous Times: A Study in Eschatological Evil* (Texarkana, Ark.: CMF, 1999), ch. 1.

[13] I highly recommend reading Josephus's *Wars of the Jews*, especially Books 4–7, in conjunction with the Olivet Discourse and Revelation. For a few examples, see my *Before Jerusalem Fell*, ch. 14.

Keep in mind that it is particularly distressing to the Jew that abominable Gentiles[14] would ultimately enter the temple of God, as do the Romans (see below). In fact, the temple's very structure has a constant reminder of the exclusion of Gentiles from its inner courts. Josephus speaks of its "dividing wall" (cp. Eph 2:14):

> When you go through these [first] cloisters, unto the second [court of the] temple, there was a partition made of stone all round, whose height was three cubits: its construction was very elegant; upon it stood pillars, at equal distances from one another, declaring the law of purity, some in Greek, and some in Roman letters, that "no foreigner should go within that sanctuary" for that second [court of the] temple was called 'the Sanctuary'" (*J.W.* 5:5:2 [193–94]; cp. 6:2:4 [125][15]).

The Jews assault Paul when they suspect that he has brought a Gentile past this wall (Acts 21:27–31; 24:6).

When the Jewish War finally comes to Jerusalem all hell breaks loose — and I mean this somewhat literally. Demonism seems to be a real factor in the Jewish War, as a comparison of Revelation 9 and Matthew 12:41–45 shows. The Idumeans stir up revolution within Jerusalem, bringing war into the Temple itself (*J.W.* 4:5): "the outer Temple was all of it overflowed with blood; and that day, as it came on, saw eight thousand five hundred dead bodies there" (*J.W.* 4:5:1 [313]). The inner strife is so bad that Josephus calls it "a sedition begotten by another sedition" which is so bad that it is "like a wild beast grown mad, which for the want of food from abroad, fell now upon eating its own flesh" (*J.W.* 5:1:1 [4]). Hence, Christ's dire warning to flee without turning back (Matt 24:16–18). Once the Roman general Titus himself begins encircling the city for the final time, it will not take him long to seal it off from the outer world (Matt 24:16–20).

As Titus begins his final march to Jerusalem, the Zealots "seize upon the inner court of the Temple, and lay their arms upon the holy gates, and over the holy fronts of that court." They even partake of the "the great abundance of what was consecrated to sacred uses" (*J.W.* 5:1:1 [4])

---

[14] Cf. Acts 10:28; 11:2-3; cf. Eph. 2:14. The Roman historian Tacitus touches on the Jewish exclusivism, when he complains of the Jews's "stubborn loyalty and ready benevolence towards brother Jews. But the rest of the world they confront with the hatred reserved for enemies. . . . They have introduced the practice of circumcision to show that they are different from others" (*Hist* 5:5).

[15] See also Philo, *Leg.* 212; Mishnah, *Mid.* 2:3; *Kelim* 1:8.

causing such an uproar that the "Temple was defiled everywhere with murders" (*J.W.* 5:1:2 [8]). They "went over all the buildings, and the Temple itself, and fell upon the priests, and those that were about the sacred offices" (*J.W.* 5:1:3 [16]).

Finally, Titus builds "a wall round about the whole city" (*J.W.* 5:12:1 [499]), causing those within the Temple to perform additional sacrilege: John of Gischala "emptied the vessels of that sacred wine and oil [cp. Rev. 6:6] which the priests kept to be poured on the burnt-offerings, and which lay in the inner court of the Temple, and distributed it among the multitude, who, in their anointing themselves and drinking, used each of them above a hin of them" (*J.W.* 5:13:6 [565]).

Soon, Titus's victory is complete: "the Romans upon the flight of the seditious into the city, and upon the burning of the holy house itself, and of all the buildings lying round about it, brought their ensigns to the Temple, and set them over against its eastern gate; and there did they offer sacrifices to them, and there did they make Titus imperator, with the greatest acclamations of joy" (*J.W.* 6:6:1 [316]). Although the "abomination of desolation" involves the destruction of Jerusalem (beginning with its encircling), it culminates in this final abominable act within in the temple itself.

Thus, the "abomination of desolation" prophecy finds complete fulfilment in AD 70 during the events leading up to and including the August/September destruction of the Temple by the armies of the Roman general Titus. The abomination of desolation is not something we should fear today. This horrible judgment of God punctuates the *end of the old covenant era and the beginning of Christ's kingdom* on earth. It does not speak of events occurring at or just after the *end of the "Church Age."*

Now we come upon another of those passages that seems particularly difficult to apply to the first-century destruction of the temple. In Matthew 24:21–22 the Lord warns his disciples of:

The Great Tribulation
In these two verses we read:

> For then there will be great tribulation, such as has not been since the beginning of the world until this time, no, nor ever shall be. And unless those days were shortened, no flesh would be saved; but for the elect's sake those days will be shortened. (Matt 24:21–22).

Futurists of all stripes almost universally deem this prophecy to be fatal to any preterist analysis. Consider the strong statements regarding Mat-

thew 24:21 by just two non-preterists. They hold that this verse precludes any possibility that AD 70 fulfilled this prophecy.
- David L. Turner recognizes that Matthew 24:16–20 focuses on the need for Jesus's disciples to "flee to the Judean hill country" because "evidently, a siege of Jerusalem is envisioned." But when explaining v 21 he writes that "the unique severity of these events is difficult to reconcile with the preterist view that this passage refers solely to the events of 70 CE."[16]
- Ed Glasscock writes that this predicts "the worst tribulation ever, which will also be worse than anything to follow. Again, the primary reason for believing this tribulation is yet future is because the destruction of Jerusalem and even the Holocaust could not be described in such superlative terms. . . . This verse clearly states that this will be a one-time-only kind of event. This expression connects with Daniel 12:1, which certainly refers to a period too great for the destruction of Jerusalem in A.D. 70."[17]

At this point I admit the statement by our Lord seems to require something quite beyond the events of AD 70 — *but only when taken out of its context*, both near (Matt 24) and far (Old Testament language). The Lord does say there "has not been [such a judgment] since the beginning of the world until this time, no, nor ever shall be." His warning speaks of the danger "no flesh would be saved." How are we to reconcile such dramatic statements to the AD 70 event?

The Preterist Interpretation

As a matter of fact, reconciliation is possible. And this is much more consistent with both the language and the expectation of Scripture than the futurist approaches to Matthew 24:1–34. Let me list five arguments against the futurist understanding of Matthew 24:21–22 each of which helps establish the preterist approach.

1. The time frame

---

[16] Turner, *Matthew*, 577, 578.
[17] Ed Glasscock, *Matthew* (MBC) (Chicago: Moody, 1997), 470–71.

Significantly, just twelve verses later Christ unambiguously declares "all these things" will befall "this generation" (Matt 24:34). And he says this in the context dealing with the destruction of the very temple then standing (Matt 23:36–24:3). We know as a matter of indisputable historical record that Titus destroys the Temple in August/September, AD 70.[18]

2. The Jewish setting

Jesus is speaking to first-century Jews living in the shadow of the temple. It is fundamentally important for us to understand this passage from the Jewish perspective in Christ's day. The Jewish War with Rome from AD 67 to 70 causes the deaths of tens of thousands of the Jews in Judea and the enslaving of untold thousands more.

The Jewish historian Flavius Josephus, an eye-witness to the Jewish War, reports that 1,100,000 Jews perished in the siege of Jerusalem (*J.W.* 6:9:3 [420]). Though many historians doubt this figure, Arndt accepts them as valid, given the flood of refugees pouring into Jerusalem as the Roman generals Vespasian and Titus drive them there by conquering the outlying regions of Palestine first.[19] J. L. von Mosheim, the great ecclesiastical historian, writes that "throughout the whole history of the human race, we meet with but few, if any, instances of slaughter and devastation at all to be compared with this."[20] Carson comments that "never [has] so high a percentage of a great city's population [been] so thoroughly and painfully exterminated and enslaved as during the Fall of Jerusalem."[21] To grasp the enormity of Jewish suffering one should read Josephus' *Jewish Wars* books four through seven, and Eusebius' *Ecclesiastical History* 3:5.

But as awful as are the Jewish loss of life and the utter devastation of "the holy city" Jerusalem, the Jews lament even more the absolute destruction of God's holy temple and the final cessation of the sacrificial system. The covenantal significance of the loss of the temple stands as the most dramatic outcome of the War. For 1000 years (since the time of Solomon) Israel's worship had centered upon her temple; for 2000 years (since the time of Abraham) Jews had worshiped God through animal

---

[18] Josephus, *J.W.* 7:1:1 [1–4].

[19] W. F. Arndt *The Gospel according to St. Luke* (St. Louis: Concordia, 1956), 421–22.

[20] John Laurence von Mosheim, *Historical Commentaries on the State of Christianity*, 2 vols., (New York: Converse, 1854), 1:125.

[21] Carson in EBC 12:501.

sacrifices: all this is over now. As E. P. Sanders notes: "It is almost impossible to make too much of the Temple in first-century Jewish Palestine."[22] After seeing the temple site shortly after its destruction, Rabbi Joshua lamented: "Woe unto us! that this, the place where the iniquities of Israel were atoned for, is laid waste!" (*Abot R. Nat.* 4). Therefore, any Jewish calamity after AD 70 pales in comparison to the redemptive-historical significance of the Temple's loss.

Josephus mourns the devastation of Jerusalem in several places employing language very close to our Lord's:

> Whereas the war which the Jews made with the Romans hath been the greatest of all those, not only that have been in our times, but, in a manner, of those that ever were heard of" (*J.W.*, Preface, 1 [1]).
> The misfortunes of all men, from the beginning of the world, if they be compared to these of the Jews, are not considerable as they were" (*J.W.*, Preface, 4 [12]).
> Neither did any other city ever suffer such miseries. . . from the beginning of the world" (*J.W.* 5:10:5 [442]).

3. The divine perspective

We must further understand the significance of AD 70 from the divine perspective. The Jewish War is God's holy judgment upon the Jews for their wickedly crucifying his Son.[23] This is clear in the ending of the Parable of the Vineyard:

> Then last of all he sent his son to them, saying, "They will respect my son." But when the vinedressers saw the son, they said among themselves, "This is the heir. Come, let us kill him and seize his inheritance." And they caught him, and cast him out of the vineyard, and killed him. Therefore, when the owner of the vineyard comes, what will he do to those vinedressers? They said to Him, "He will destroy those wicked men miserably, and lease his vineyard to other vinedressers who will render to him the fruits in their seasons" (Matt 21:37-41).

---

[22] E. P. Sanders *The Historical Figure of Jesus* (London: Penguin, 1993), 262.

[23] The New Testament strongly emphasizes first-century Jewish culpability for the crucifixion of Christ: Acts 2:22-23; Acts 3:13–15a; Acts 5:30; 7:52; 1 Thess. 2:14–15. They demand that the Romans crucify Him: Matt 20:18–19; 27:11–25; Mark 10:33; 15:1; Luke 18:32; 23:1–2; John 18:28–31; 19:12, 15; Acts 3:13; Acts 4:26–27.

Luke 19:41-44 is also relevant:

> Now as he drew near, he saw the city and wept over it, saying, "If you had known, even you, especially in this your day, the things that make for your peace! But now they are hidden from your eyes. For the days will come upon you when your enemies will build an embankment around you, surround you and close you in on every side, and level you, and your children within you, to the ground; and they will not leave in you one stone upon another, because you did not know the time of your visitation."

4. The Noahic flood

What is more, just a few verses after Matthew 24:21–22 the Lord mentions the Noahic Flood (vv. 38–39), which was global, covering the entire world (Gen 7:19–20; 8:5). It destroys the *entire* world except for one family: "the patience of God kept waiting in the days of Noah, during the construction of the ark, in which a few, that is, eight persons, were brought safely through the water" (1 Pet 3:20). God "did not spare the ancient world, but preserved Noah, a preacher of righteousness, with seven others, when He brought a flood upon the world of the ungodly" (2 Pet 2:5; cp. 2 Pet 3:6). Even dispensationalists' statements see their great tribulation as stopping far short of leaving only *one family* alive. Jesus has no problem in employing dramatic hyperbole to explain the destruction of Jerusalem and the temple — even in a discourse where he mentions an even greater catastrophe, the Noahic Deluge.

5. Prophetic parlance

Christ's dramatic language in describing Jerusalem's fall as absolutely unique (never before / never again) is common stock-in-trade language, a proverbial expression from the Old Testament prophetic writings. Lane comments on Mark 13:19 (the parallel verse to Matt 24:21):

> The severity of the distress that will accompany the destruction of Jerusalem is vividly suggested through Semitic hyperbole. Characteristically, oracles of judgment are couched in language that is universal and radical. The intention is to indicate that through human events God intervenes powerfully to modify the course of history. The entire world feels the vibrations of that intervention.[24]

---

[24] William L. Lane, *The Gospel of Mark* (NICNT) (Grand Rapids: Eerdmans, 1974), 471.

This is most interesting to the preterist, for it dismantles a fundamental argument of the futurist. The Old Testament records several such statements that support our view that the language is hyperbolic.

Regarding the woe of the tenth plague upon Egypt, the Scripture states: "Then there shall be a great cry throughout all the land of Egypt, *such as was not like it before, nor shall be like it again*" (Exo 11:6). According to dispensationalists the future great tribulation affects the entire earth; consequently, it affects Egypt. But Exodus 11:6 declares that Egypt will *never again* experience such a terrible event as the tenth plague — which occurs 1500 hundred years before Christ speaks. Yet the future great tribulation is supposed to be the worst ever for everyone — including Egyptians. Clearly the Exodus statement is dramatic hyperbole. Thus, the same may be true of Matthew 24:21.

In a prophecy regarding the Babylonian captivity and the destruction of Jerusalem God employs language reminiscent of Christ's: "And I will do among you what *I have never done, and the like of which I will never do again*, because of all your abominations" (Eze 5:9). Even dispensationalists admit this prophecy is about the Babylonian captivity of the distant past.[25] And this is specifically about Jerusalem, which is very prominent in the Matthew 24 passage. Clearly the Daniel statement is dramatic hyperbole. Thus, the same may be true of Matthew 24:21.

In 2 Kings 18:5 we read of Hezekiah: "He trusted in the Lord, the God of Israel; so that after him there was none like him among all the kings of Judah, nor among those who were before him." This surely does not mean that Hezekiah was the *only* king ever to trust in the Lord to such an extent. We know this is not the case because just five chapters later we read of Josiah in 2 Kings 23:25: "And before him there was no king like him who turned to the Lord with all his heart and with all his soul and with all his might, according to all the law of Moses; nor did any like him arise after him." Which was the more trusting and faithful king: Hezekiah or Josiah? The uniqueness language is applied to *both* kings; it is dramatic hyperbole.

Thus we can see that the unique-event language is common parlance in the Scriptures. We must not interpret it in a woodenly literal manner.

---

[25] Walvoord, *Prophecy Knowledge Handbook*, 160. J. Dwight Pentecost, *Thy Kingdom Come* (Wheaton, Ill.: Victor, 1990), 180. Charles H. Dyer, "Ezekiel," in John F. Walvoord and Roy B. Zuck, eds., *The Bible Knowledge Commentary: Old Testament* (Wheaton, Ill.: Victor, 1985), 1236.

This historical episode is so destructive that the Lord warns: "unless those days had been cut short, no life would have been saved; but for the sake of the elect those days shall be cut short" (Matt 24:22). This is speaking of physical "salvation," not spiritual (see the concept of rescue from physical danger in Matt 8:25; 14:30; 27:40–42). The "no flesh" statement often means simply "no one," meaning no one in a particular historical context (e.g., Luke 3:6; Acts 2:17).

False Christs and False Prophets (Matt 24:23—28)

At this point Jesus returns to a previous theme, but accentuates it. In Matthew 24:23–28 we again hear him warning about false prophets, a warning reminiscent of verses 5 and 11. But now he explains how these men can mislead so many: they "will show great signs":

> Then if anyone says to you, "Behold, here is the Christ," or "There He is," do not believe him. For false Christs and false prophets will arise and will show great signs and wonders, so as to mislead, if possible, even the elect. Behold, I have told you in advance.

The problem of false prophets and Christ is so serious in the first century that the Lord reiterates his warning against falling for escape promises by these self-deluded enthusiasts.

Our will to survive is one of our most basic instincts: we tend to flee to avoid danger. As Josephus says of the false prophecies during the Jewish War: "Now, a man that is in adversity does easily comply with such promises; for when such a seducer makes him believe that he shall be delivered from those miseries which oppress him, then it is that the patient is full of hopes of such deliverance" (*J.W.* 6:5:2 [287]) Our will to live is God-created in that he "has put eternity in their hearts" (Eccl 3:11). With the onset of the great tribulation, anxiety will overcome many; false messianic expectations and fraudulent signs could therefore easily tempt them.

False Christs

Unfounded hope for escape during the perilous times of the first century is fertile ground for messianic expectations. So Christ expressly warns his followers against succumbing to such. I have already provided biblical evidence for false Christs arising during the apostolic era; let me now bring in some extra-biblical evidence. These data — as every other in Matthew 24:1–36 — have a direct historical relevance to the pre-AD 70 era.

In John Lightfoot's encyclopedic research in Jewish Talmudic literature, we find records of rabbinic interpretations that fuel false Messianic fervor in the first century. Isaiah 56:7 reads: "Before she travailed, she gave birth; before her pain came, she delivered a male child." Based on this, the rabbis argue "that the Messias should be manifested before the destruction of the city."[26] But Jesus' followers are not to fall for such.

Micah 5:3 reads: "Therefore He shall give them up, until the time that she who is in labor has given birth; then the remnant of his brethren shall return to the children of Israel." From this the rabbis deduce that "the Son of David will not come, till the wicked empire [of the Romans] shall have spread itself over all the world nine months." Clearly a Messianic hope is in the air as the fateful events of the AD 60s unfold on the scene of history.

False signs

Josephus records for us the following incidents that occur before the outbreak of the Jewish War with Rome.

> There was also another body of wicked men gotten together, not so impure in their actions, but more wicked in their intentions, who laid waste the happy state of the city [Jerusalem] no less than did these murderers. These were such men as deceived and deluded the people under pretense of divine inspiration, but were for procuring innovations and changes of the government; and these prevailed with the multitude to act like madmen, and went before them into the wilderness, as pretending that God would there shew them the signal of liberty. (J.W. 2:13:4 [258–59])

• • •

> There was an Egyptian false prophet that did the Jews more mischief than the former; for he was a cheat, and pretended to be a prophet also, and got together thirty thousand men that were deluded by him; these he led round about from the wilderness to the mount which was called the Mount of Olives, and was ready to break into Jerusalem by force from that place. (J.W. 2:13:5 [261–62])

• • •

---

[26] Babylonian Yoma, fol. 10.1. Cited in: John Lightfoot, *A Commentary on the New Testament from the Talmud and Hebraica*, 4 vols., (Peabody, Mass.: Hendrickson, rep. 1989 [1658]), 1:318-319.

A false prophet was the occasion of these people's destruction, who had made a public proclamation in the city that very day, that God commanded them to get up upon the temple, and there should received miraculous signs of their deliverance. Now, there was then a great number of false prophets suborned by the tyrants to impose upon the people, who denounced this to them, that they should wait for deliverance from God. (*J.W.* 6:5:2 [285–86])

The Lord cautions his disciples: "If therefore they say to you, 'Behold, He is in the wilderness,' do not go forth, or, 'Behold, He is in the inner rooms,' do not believe them" (Matt 24:26). We must recall Josephus' report in *Jewish Wars* 2:13:5 [261–62] cited above that recorded an episode in which an Egyptian false prophet arose in the wilderness claiming a great deliverance.

Jesus dismisses such by stating that when he physically comes again to the earth, it will be an unmistakable event: "For just as the lightning comes from the east, and flashes even to the west, so shall the coming of the Son of Man be" (Matt 24:27). The "for" (*gar*) here shows that he is giving the reason why his disciples should not think he is off in some wilderness or in an inner room somewhere. When he does return it will be as visible and dramatic as lightning flashing.[27]

So again, we see how the prophecies of Matthew 24 find fulfillment in the first century. In that these prophecies are for that era (Matt 24:34), why should we opt for a futurist approach to the matter?

A carcass for eagles

Having contrasted his dramatic coming in the second advent with the metaphorical coming in AD 70, in Matthew 24:28 Jesus returns to the AD 70 judgment. Here we read of birds of prey consuming the carcasses: "For

---

[27] I should note that my interpretation of this verse has changed recently. In earlier works (*Perilous Times*; *The Great Tribulation: Past or Future?*) I argued that the lightning flash could refer to his spiritual judgment-coming in AD 70. This is certainly possible, given the dramatic nature of prophetic language. But I now reject that view because of grammatical and contextual reasons. The "for" (grammar) in v 27 clearly gives the reason (context) why they should not expect that he may be off somewhere in a wilderness. His physical return will be visible to all. After all, the original question (24:3) shows the disciples' conflating of the two events: AD 70 and the second advent. Just a few verses later (24:36ff) Jesus will begin focusing on that more glorious event.

wherever the carcass is, there the eagles will be gathered together" (NKJV).

This statement speaks of the dreadful devastation Rome wreaks upon Israel in the Jewish War, particularly in the final five month siege and destruction. The furious soldiers who cruelly ravage the people will destroy the population, the city, and the temple. Josephus often mentions the rage of the Roman troops. For instance: "As for the legions that came running thither, neither any persuasions nor any threatenings could restrain their violence, but each one's own passion was his commander at this time" (*J.W.* 6:4:6 [257]). And: "the army now having no victims either for slaughter or plunder, through lack of all objects on which to vent their rage" (*J.W.* 7:1:1 [1]). He further notes that

> while the holy house was on fire, every thing was plundered that came to hand, and ten thousand of those that were caught were slain; nor was there a commiseration of any age, or any reverence of gravity, but children, and old men, and profane persons, and priests were all slain in the same manner; so that this war went round all sorts of men, and brought them to destruction. (*J.W.* 6:5:1 [271])

The image is familiar enough to an agrarian people: an ugly, rotting corpse blanketed by bickering birds of prey (see: Gen 40:19; 1 Kgs 14:11; 16:4; 21:24; Isa 18:6; Jer 7:3; 15:3; 16:4; 19:7; 34:20). God even employs this imagery in warning of his covenant curse upon Israel for her rebellion: ""And your carcasses shall be food to all birds of the sky and to the beasts of the earth, and there shall be no one to frighten them away" (Deut 28:26 [cf. 28:15]; cp. Psa 79:2; Jer 7:33; 12:9; 16:4; 19:7; 34:20). In a well-known vision in Scripture a dead body symbolizes rebellious Israel: the vision of the dry bones in Ezekiel 37.[28] She is morally, spiritually, and covenantally dead in the eyes of God.

Before giving his Olivet Discourse Christ symbolically portrays his death-dealing wrath on Israel by cursing the fig tree (Matt 21:19–20). Shortly thereafter he speaks a parable about his rejection by Israel, which the Pharisees foolishly agree should be recompensed by the destruction of those responsible (21: 33–41). Then he speaks of himself as the "Stone which the builders rejected" (Matt 21:42). After this he says: "And who-

---

[28] The mysterious reference to Michael and Satan contending for the body of Moses should probably be understood in this manner (Jude 9), as many reformed commentators note. The body of Moses is the nation of Israel, much like the body of Christ is the Church.

ever falls on this stone will be broken; but on whomever it falls, it will grind him to powder" (21:44). Ultimately, upon Israel comes "all the righteous blood shed on the earth, from the blood of righteous Abel to the blood of Zechariah, son of Berechiah, whom you murdered between the temple and the altar" (23:35).

This judgment comes through God's providential instrument, the Roman army (cf. Matt 22:7). Even Josephus recognizes this when he urges the Jews to surrender to the Romans after he himself is captured by them: "God is fled out of his sanctuary, and stands on the side of those against whom you fight" (*J.W.* 5:9:4 [412]). A little later he warns: "It is God, therefore, it is God himself who is brining on this fire, to purge that city and temple by means of the Romans and is going to pluck up this city, which is full of your pollutions" (*J.W.* 6:2:1 [110]). Israel is judicially dead; the Roman armies will devour her carcass. This is why Jesus weeps over Jerusalem (23:37). This results from God leaving her house desolate (23:38). The Spirit of God, which is her life, departs from her. Consequently, God will totally destroy her capital city and holy temple.

To better grasp the impact of t his image, we must understand that the Scriptures view the human body as a wondrous creation by God, inspiring awe among God's people (Psa 139:13–16; Eccl 10:5). Because God wonderfully fashions man's body (Gen 2:7), his people treat it with the utmost respect, carefully preparing it for burial (John 19:40; cp. Eccl 6:3[29]). Only the bodies of vile sinners are denied proper preparation for burial, having their corpses cremated instead (Gen 23:19; Lev 21:9;[30] 1 Sam 31:12). The death-dealing judgment of God on covenant rebellion often causes a tragic loss of burial arrangements, resulting in animals devouring the bodies of the deceased. Again, this is an aspect of covenantal curse (Deut 28:26; cp. Psa 79:3; Jer 14:6).

Now why does the Lord portray this judgment with *eagles* preying upon the carcass? It is interesting that he chooses the word "eagle" (*aetos*) here. He could choose a more generic term such as *orneon* ("fowl"), such as John employs in a similar context in Revelation 19:21. Or *peteinon* which usually speaks of wild birds (Acts 10:12; 11:6; Rom 1:23; Jms 3:7),

---

[29] See also: Gen. 23:19; 47:30; 49:29; 50:5; Jer. 16:4. Cf. Tacitus, *The Histories* 5:6: "Rather than cremate their dead, they prefer to bury them." Cf. Mishnah, *Shabbath* 23:5; *Sanhedrin* 6:5.

[30] The burning of these adulteresses would occur after they have died by stoning or some other such means.

and is a term Jesus frequently uses (Matt 6:26; 8:20; 13:4, 32; Luke 12:24). Or even *korax* which represents a flesh-eating bird, the raven (Luke 12:24). Instead, he selects a term that reminds us of the symbol of the Roman Empire. Josephus comments on the marching order of the legions:

> Then came the ensigns encompassing the eagle [*aeton*], which is at the head of every Roman legion, the king, and the strongest of all birds, which seems to them a signal of dominion, and an omen that they shall conquer all against whom they march; these sacred ensigns are followed by the trumpeters." (*J.W.* 3:6:2 [123]; cp. Suetonius, *Galba* 13)

• • •

> All these came before the engines; and after these engines came the tribunes and the leaders of the cohorts, with their select bodies; after these came the ensigns, with the eagle [*aieton*]; and before those ensigns came the trumpeters belonging to them." (*J.W.* 5:2:1 [48])

Interestingly, the word *aetos* ("eagle") appears in the covenant curse passage in the Septuagint: "The Lord will bring a nation against you from afar, from the end of the earth, as the eagle swoops down, a nation whose language you shall not understand" (Deut 28:49). This term appears often in the Old Testament as describing eagles, rather than vultures (Psa 103:5; Isa 40:31; Lam 4:19; Eze 10:14; 17:3; Hos 8:1; Oba 4).

As I noted previously, Josephus records the ultimate act that lies behind the imagery here: "The Romans, now that the rebels had fled to the city, and the sanctuary itself and all around it were in flames, carried their standards into the temple court and, setting them up opposite the eastern gate, there sacrificed to them, and with rousing acclamations hailed Titus as imperator" (*J.W.* 6:6:1 [316]). As already noted the Roman ensigns bear the eagle as the symbol of Rome. In fact, to the Roman legionaries these were "sacred emblems" (*J.W.* 3:6:2 [124]).

Thus, as Jerusalem collapses to her "death" the marauding armies of Rome pour into the city and into the temple to devour the corpse. Jerusalem is so stripped of her valuables that Josephus writes: "So glutted with plunder were the troops, one and all, that throughout Syria the standard of gold was depreciated to half its former value" (*J.W.* 6:6:1 [317]). The image of eagles descending upon a corpse is most apropos in these circumstances.

Chapter 7
THE COMING OF THE END
Matthew 24:29–31

In this chapter we finally enter the section of Jesus' Olivet Discourse where we witness the coming of the end of the temple. Given the dramatic redemptive-historical significance of this event, Jesus casts it in highly-wrought symbolic imagery. This section contains portions of the prophecy that are the most difficult to apprehend by our Western, scientific minds. In fact, this section contains material that liberals often use to argue that Christ's prophecy was mistaken — because they attempt to interpret it literally rather than according to the Old Testament prophetic pattern.[1]

The Collapsing Universe (Matt 24:49)
In Matthew 24:29 the Lord states:

> But immediately after the tribulation of those days the sun will be darkened, and the moon will not give its light, and the stars will fall from the sky, and the powers of the heavens will be shaken.

A quick reading of this statement seems to undermine the preterist approach I have been presenting. Indeed, this is one of the leading verses that dispensationalists use to rebut preterism. And certainly if we were to interpret this passage in a strictly literal sense, it would be difficult to associate these prophetic events with AD 70. But looks are deceiving. I will show that the prophecy here *can* easily be interpreted in terms of the AD 70 judgment on Israel.

As we begin considering this verse I must once again mention the all-important time-designate that controls the passage. *Just five verses after this statement Jesus emphatically declares: "Truly I say to you, this generation will not pass away until all these things take place" (Matt 24:34).*

But how shall we understand verse 29? Rather than interpreting it in a woodenly-literal manner, we must interpret it biblically and covenant-

---

[1] See especially R. C. Sproul, *The Last Days according to Jesus: When Did Jesus Say He Would Return?* (Grand Rapids: Baker, 1998). Sproul argues against the liberal interpretation and defends a preterist understanding of the dramatic imagery.

ally. That is, we should let Scripture interpret Scripture. Since I have been demonstrating that the whole preceding context suggests that this passage speaks of the AD 70 collapse of geo-political Israel, I will now note the biblical warrant for speaking of Israel's national catastrophe in terms that sound like cosmic destruction.

Temporal notes

Before we even begin considering the dramatic language itself, we must note Jesus' declaring that these events will occur "*immediately* after the tribulation of those days" (Matt 24:29a). The word "immediately" (Gk.: *eutheos)* occurs thirteen times in Matthew and always signifies something occurring very soon after a preceding event. For instance, this word is used when Jesus calls Simon and Andrew and Matthew reports that "they immediately left the nets, and followed him."[2]

I must make two relevant observations in this regard: First, everything I have presented through our last several chapters demands that Jesus is dealing with the AD 70 judgment. Second, the immediacy of this statement forbids us from supposing that these events have to do with any long term consideration, such as appears in the latter half of the Discourse (and regards the second advent). For that event is spoken of as distant (Matt 24:48; 25:5, 19), whereas this event will follow immediately.

All of this fits perfectly within the Discourse's flowing context. Note the following: (1) The disciples' leading question seeks an answer to "*when* will these things be" (Matt 24:3). (2) Jesus' warns them not to let anyone mislead them as to when these things will occur (24:4). (3) He states of the early, more general signs: "that is *not yet* the end" (24:6). (4) He declares that the earlier signs are really only "the *beginning* of birth pangs" (24:8). (5) He also states that "those days shall be cut short" (24:22). The near term temporal expectation of the event he is introducing is very important.

But now let us consider his:

Dramatic language

How shall we understand Jesus' dramatic language itself? This cosmic-distress imagery speaks of God exercising his wrath against his earthly

---

[2] See the other uses of "immediately": Matt 4:20, 22; 8:3; 13:5; 14:22, 31; 20:34; 21:2; 25:15; 26:49, 74; 27:48.

enemies. We see similar "earth-shaking" language in Deborah and Barak's song at the defeat of the Canaanite king Jabin (Jdg 4:24 – 5:1):

> Lord, when Thou didst go out from Seir, / When Thou didst march from the field of Edom, / The earth quaked, the heavens also dripped, / Even the clouds dripped water. / The mountains quaked at the presence of the Lord, / This Sinai, at the presence of the Lord, the God of Israel. (Jdg 5:4–5)

Basically such imagery indicates that the Creator of the world is judging kings of the earth, showing them to be puny. We will see in the next verse that Jesus explains this by representing himself as coming from heaven on the clouds (Matt 24:30).

More importantly though, the Lord's language strongly echoes Isaiah 13 where the prophet is prophesying Babylon's collapse in the Old Testament. Before I cite the relevant verses, though, I would point out that Isaiah is definitely speaking of the fall of Babylon. He *opens* his prophecy with these words: "The oracle concerning Babylon which Isaiah the son of Amoz saw" (Isa 13:1). And just *after* the relevant portion of the prophecy he states:

> Behold, I am going to stir up the Medes against them, / Who will not value silver or take pleasure in gold. . . . And Babylon, the beauty of kingdoms, the glory of the Chaldeans' pride, / Will be as when God overthrew Sodom and Gomorrah. (Isa 13:17, 19)

So now, how does Isaiah describe Old Testament Babylon's historic fall? By using cosmic destruction language:

> For the stars of heaven and their constellations / Will not flash forth their light; / The sun will be dark when it rises, / And the moon will not shed its light. . . . Therefore I shall make the heavens tremble, / And the earth will be shaken from its place / At the fury of the Lord of hosts / In the day of His burning anger. (Isa 13:10, 13)

This matches quite closely with Jesus' prophecy in Matthew 24. Thus, we should not dismiss the possibility that Jesus is referring to the historical fall of Jerusalem since God's prophets use such language in prophesying historical Old Testament judgments.

Indeed, Isaiah also describes the fall of historical Edom with similar imagery:

> So their slain will be thrown out, / And their corpses will give off their stench, / And the mountains will be drenched with their blood. / And all the host of heaven will wear away, / And the sky will be rolled up like a scroll; / All their hosts will also wither away / As a leaf withers from the

vine, / Or as one withers from the fig tree. / For My sword is satiated in heaven, / Behold it shall descend for judgment upon Edom, / And upon the people whom I have devoted to destruction. (Isa 34:3–5)

Elsewhere Ezekiel describes the fall of Egypt in history in parallel terms:

Son of man, take up a lamentation over Pharaoh king of Egypt, and say to him, "You compared yourself to a young lion of the nations, / Yet you are like the monster in the seas; / And you burst forth in your rivers, / And muddied the waters with your feet, / And fouled their rivers. . . . And when I extinguish you, / I will cover the heavens, and darken their stars; / I will cover the sun with a cloud, / And the moon shall not give its light. / All the shining lights in the heavens / I will darken over you / And will set darkness on your land," / Declares the Lord God. (Eze 32:2, 7–8)

What is more, Jeremiah also applies this vivid poetic language to *Israel's* Old Testament judgment under Babylon:

In that time it will be said to this people and to Jerusalem, "A scorching wind from the bare heights in the wilderness in the direction of the daughter of My people — not to winnow, and not to cleanse. . . .I looked on the earth, and behold, it was formless and void; / And to the heavens, and they had no light. / I looked on the mountains, and behold, they were quaking, / And all the hills moved to and fro." (Jer 4:11, 23–24)

Similarly the prophet Joel prophesies Israel's Old Testament judgment:

Blow a trumpet in Zion, And sound an alarm on My holy mountain! / Let all the inhabitants of the land tremble, / For the day of the Lord is coming; / Surely it is near. . . . Before them the earth quakes, / The heavens tremble, / The sun and the moon grow dark, / And the stars lose their brightness." (Joel 2:1, 10)

Such imagery, then, indicates that the God of the heavens (the Creator of the sun, moon, and stars) is moving in judgment against an earthly nation. When a national government collapses in war and upheaval Scripture often poetically portrays it "as a cosmic catastrophe — an undoing of Creation."[3]

Consequently, we may easily apply Matthew 24:29 to the destruction of Jerusalem in AD 70. Christ draws the imagery in his prophecy from Old Testament judgment passages that sound as if they are world-ending events. And in a sense it is "the end of the world" for those nations God judges. So is it with Israel in AD 70.

---

[3] Charles H. Dyer, "Jeremiah," *BKC: OT*, 1135.

The Son of Man in Heaven (Matt 24:30)
Now how shall we interpret the next verse in this dramatic discourse?

> And then the sign of the Son of Man will appear in the sky, and then all the tribes of the earth will mourn, and they will see the Son of Man coming on the clouds of the sky with power and great glory. (Matt 24:30)

Once again, despite initial appearances this statement also applies to the AD 70 destruction of the temple. Though we may easily see how futurists apply this to the second advent, a closer consideration of several elements within it will show how nicely it fits into the preterist understanding of the whole passage.

Grammatical considerations
Here I will follow the translation of Matthew 24:30 as found in the Authorized Version (KJV) and the American Standard Version (1901). The key phrase follows the Greek word order more closely and translates an important word more contextually: "Then shall appear the sign of the Son of Man in *heaven*" (cp. ESV, N.B.).

An interlinear Greek translation of Matthew 24:30 reads as follows:

> kai tote phanesetai to semeion tou huiou tou anthropou en ourano
> and then shall appear the sign of the son of man in heaven

In fact, this is the translation presented in Marshall's *The Interlinear NASB-NIV Parallel New Testament in Greek and English*: "And then will appear the sign of the Son of man in heaven."

It is important to note that "the sign" is what "shall appear."[4] It is misleading to understand the phrase as meaning "then shall appear the Son of Man in the sky." The Son of Man does not appear; the *sign* appears.[5] Then Christ defines what the sign signifies: it is the sign that the Son of Man is now in heaven. That is, this sign (whatever it is) will signify that Jesus is in heaven above — despite the Jewish authorities and rulers of the temple killing him (Matt 16:21; 20:18; 26:3–4, 59, 65–66; 27:20), sealing his tomb (27:62–66), and denying his resurrection (28:11–15).

---

[4] Be aware: the Greek *phaino* ("appear") may indicate "perceive, recognize," and not just "personally appear." See: 2 Cor 13:7; Luke 24:11.

[5] Technically this translation of the "sign of the Son of Man" is known as an objective genitive. Thus, in an expansive translation could be read to mean: "the sign which shows the Son of Man."

Remember that the Lord is responding to his disciples' two questions: (1) "When will these things be"; and (2) "what will be the sign of Your coming and of the end of the age" (Matt 24:3). Unfortunately, as noted in chapter 3 above, the disciples frequently misunderstand Jesus' teaching. Thus, even though he is now nearing the end of over three years of teaching them, their two questions betray their eschatological confusion. They misconstrue matters by uniting the destruction of the temple with the end of the world.

As France well notes: "the disciples had asked for a 'sign' of the *parousia* and the end of the age, but Jesus will give no such sign because the *parousia* will be sudden and unexpected (vv. 27, 36–44)."[6] He does not give them a sign for the second advent event *because*: it will be signless. After all, even Jesus himself denies knowing when that will be (Matt 24:36). Hence, we might say over against the disciples: what God has separated let no man join together.

What Christ teaches here is extremely important, not only regarding Matthew's unfolding story-line, but also regarding the divinely-ordained flow of redemptive history. The Temple's final destruction (the main topic of the Discourse, Matt 23:38–24:3) serves as *the* sign that the Son of Man is in heaven. Gibbs expresses it well: "That sign will be the destruction of Jerusalem, for in that event the implied reader perceives the truth that God has vindicated Jesus over his enemies, the religious leaders of Israel."[7]

Let's look at little more closely at the "sign."

The smoking temple

In effect "the sign" of Jesus' vindication is the smoke of the burning temple (and probably Jerusalem itself, Matt 22:7). Matthew 24:30 appears to refer to the same event as Acts 2:19, which reads:

> I will grant wonders in the sky above, / And signs on the earth beneath, / Blood, and fire, and vapor of smoke.[8]

These words were spoken to the "men of Judea, and all you who live in Jerusalem" (Acts 2:14), to the "men of Israel" (2:22), to "the house of

---

[6] R. T. France, *The Gospel of Matthew* (NICNT) (Grand Rapids: Eerdmans, 2007), 926.

[7] Jeffrey A. Gibbs, *Jerusalem and Parousia: Jesus' Eschatological Discourse in Matthew's Gospel* (St. Louis: Concordia Academic Press, 2000), 199.

[8] Note also the parallel of Acts 2:20 with Matt 24:29.

Israel" (2:36). The elements highlighted — the "blood, and fire, and vapor of smoke" — mark the total collapse of Jerusalem and serve as the sign that the Jesus is at God's right hand.

After citing these words Peter condemns Israel for rejecting and killing Christ: "this Man . . . you nailed to a cross by the hands of godless men and put Him to death" (Acts 2:23). Yet despite Israel's attempt to destroy him, "God raised him up" (2:24)" so that now he has "been exalted to the right hand of God" (2:33). The coming "blood, and fire, and vapor of smoke" begins the process of fulfilling the messianic promise: "sit at My right hand, / until I make Thine enemies a footstool for Thy feet" (2:34b–35). Israel will be his first enemy to fall beneath his feet.

As Peter closes his Pentecost sermon he warns: "Therefore let all the house of Israel know for certain that God has made Him both Lord and Christ — this Jesus whom you crucified" (Acts 2:36). When his audience asks: "brethren, what shall we do?", he responds that they must repent (2:38) so that they might "be saved from this perverse generation" (2:40).

Josephus records that fateful day when the very temple of God goes up in flames:

> But as for that house, God had, for certain, long ago doomed it to the fire; and now that fatal day was come, according to the revolution of ages; it was the tenth day of the month Lous, [Ab,] upon which it was formerly burnt by the king of Babylon; although these flames took their rise from the Jews themselves. (J.W. 6:4:5 [250])

The fire was so vigorous that he reports: "The flame was also carried a long way, and made an echo, together with the groans of those that were slain; and because this hill was high, and the works at the temple were very great, one would have thought the whole city had been on fire" (J.W. 6:5:1 [272]). He then laments: "one would have thought that the hill itself, on which the temple stood, was seething hot, as full of fire on every part of it" (J.W. 6:5:1 [275]).

Interestingly, smoke serves as a sign for Israel's armies in the Old Testament: "Now the appointed signal between the men of Israel and the men in ambush was that they would make a great cloud of smoke rise up from the city" (Jdgs 20:38). In Scripture the billowing of smoke clouds from a scene of judgment often serves as evidence of that judgment (Gen 19:28; Josh 18:20; 20:40; Psa 37:20; Isa 14:31; 34:10; Rev 14:11; 18:9).

In another context employing slightly different terminology, Christ tells the high priest and the Sanhedrin who condemn Him: "I say to you, hereafter you will see the Son of Man sitting at the right hand of the

Power, and coming on the clouds of heaven" (Matt 26:64). In the smoky destruction of Jerusalem these Jewish leaders should see the Son of Man's position of power that brings about his cloud-judgment.

Thus, the fiery destruction of the temple is a sign signifying that the Son of Man is in heaven. Despite the disbelief of the Jews (John 6:32–42) who seek signs from heaven (Matt 16:1; Mark 8:11; Luke 11:16), Christ is from heaven. He came from heaven (John 3:13, 31; 6:42; 17:5) and ascends back to it (Mark 16:19; Luke 24:51; John 14:2, 4). The era of racial focus (the Jews), geographical delimitation (the Promised Land), and typological ministry (the Temple and its services) is fading away: "When He said, 'A new covenant,' He has made the first obsolete. But whatever is becoming obsolete and growing old is ready to disappear" (Heb 8:13; cp. John 4:21– 23; Heb 12:27–28). The destruction of the Temple is the final, conclusive sign that the Son of Man is in heaven from where he exercises his Lordship over Israel.

Heaven above

The Greek word for "heaven" here is *ouranos*, which may be translated either "heaven" (the abode of God) or "sky" (the cloudy atmosphere above the ground). Here it is best to translate it as "heaven." This fits better with the redemptive historical significance of the earthly Temple's removal and the ascending to heaven of the True Temple, Jesus Christ (cf. John 2:18–22; cp. Matt 12:6).

If one disputes this translation, however, the preterist utility of the verse still remains. Suppose we translate the verse: "then shall appear the sign of the Son of man in the sky." In this case we would apply *the sign in the sky* to the *place where the smoke ascends* from Jerusalem's smoldering remains. That is, if the verse is not informing us of the ultimate reality that Jerusalem's destruction is proof the Son of Man is in heaven, then it would be teaching that the smoke-sign in the sky is an indication of his visitation of Jerusalem in wrath. Either way, preterism sufficiently accounts for Matthew 24:30a, though the initial translation is much preferred.

Consider one of the options Dallas Seminary's commentary suggests: "Exactly what the sign of the Son of Man will be is unknown . . . . Some believe the sign may involve the heavenly city, New Jerusalem, which may descend at this time and remain as a satellite city suspended over the earthly city Jerusalem throughout the Millennium (Rev. 21:2–3)."[9] This is a strange interpretation, to say the least.

The "tribes of the land"
In Matthew 24:30b we read:

> Then all the tribes of the earth will mourn, and they will see the Son of Man coming on the clouds of heaven with power and great glory.

To unpack the meaning of this statement we must first ask: Who are these "tribes of the earth"?

As with the word *ouranos* (mentioned above), so the word *ge* (translated "earth") may express several different concepts. But basically the word may have either a general referent: *the earth, the world*. Or it may have a specific referent: *a particular land area, a nation*.

Here *ge* seems to be referring to a particular land: Israel. Matthew often uses *ge* to mean Israel, the Promised Land. We see this when he speaks of "the *land* of Judah" (Matt 2:6) and "the *land* of Israel" (2:20, 21). This also appears to be its meaning in Matthew 27:45: "Now from the sixth hour darkness fell upon all *the land* until the ninth hour." Jesus' death causes darkness to befall "the land" where his death occurs, i.e., Israel. This also fits the Discourse's context which focuses on the "holy place" (Matt 24:15) which is in Israel (the Land) and on Judea which is a region within Israel (the Land).

Besides this evidence we must note that the only other time "tribes" appears in Matthew is at 19:28. There they specifically refer to the tribes of *Israel*: "Truly I say to you, that you who have followed Me, in the regeneration when the Son of Man will sit on His glorious throne, you also shall sit upon twelve thrones, judging the twelve *tribes of Israel*."

That he refers to "the tribes" of the Land reinforces this view in that it is a common designate for the tribal structure of Israel.[10] The Septuagint "with few exceptions . . . has *phule* ("tribe"), so that this becomes a

---

[9] Barbieri, "Matthew" (BKC:NT), 78. J. Dwight Pentecost holds this strange conception of the New Jerusalem, see: J. Dwight Pentecost, *Things to Come: A Study in Biblical Eschatology* (Grand Rapids: Zondervan, 1958), 577–580.

[10] Gen. 49:28; Exo. 24:4; Eze. 47:13; Matt 19:28; Luke 22:30; Acts 26:7; Rev. 21:12.

fixed term for the tribal system of Israel."[11] Indeed, the Old Testament text from which Christ draws this wording shows the tribes of Israel are in view (cf. Zech 12:10–14). Furthermore, the New Testament itself generally applies "tribe" to the people of Israel (Luke 2:36; 22:30; Acts 13:21; 26:7; Rom 11:1; Phil 3:5; Heb 7:13–14; Jms 1:1).

So then, in his statement recorded in Matthew 24:30 Jesus is referring to the tribes of the Land of Israel. But now what about:

The mourning of the tribes

The word "mourning" (Gk.: *kopto*) can signify either the weeping of repentance (as it does in the prophecy to which Christ alludes, Zech 12:10) or the wailing of lamentation. Which does it signify here in Matthew 24:30? It surely speaks of lamentation, as we may discern from the following observations.

First, the whole passage in which the "mourning" is set speaks of judgment — even such as the world has never before experienced (Matt 24:21). It refers to war (24:6), earthquakes (24:7), tribulation (24:9), betrayals (24:10), abomination (24:15), desperate flight (24:16), woe (24:19), and a "corpse" (24:28). Second, the particular place of terror will be in "the holy place" (24:15) which requires flight from Judea (24:16). Any Jew who witnesses the desolation of the holy place and must flee from Judea must surely lament what is befalling his beloved land.

Third, the cosmic-destruction imagery signifies chaos and destruction that would lead to lamentation in great fear (Matt 24:29). Fourth, the sign that the Son of Man is in heaven speaks of judgment as it most definitely does in Matthew 26:64. There Jesus responds to the Sanhedrin who are about to condemn him to death: "You have said it yourself; nevertheless I tell you, hereafter you shall see the Son of Man sitting at the right hand of Power, and coming on the clouds of heaven." In fact, sitting on the right hand of power indicates the vindication of Jesus when God puts "thine enemies beneath Thy feet" (22:44).

Clearly then, Jesus warns of Israel's judgment and her lamentation under it. Thus, mourning will befall the Jewish tribes in Israel; they will endure the brunt of God's wrath and judgment for their rejection of Christ. After their fearful flight from Judea they shall mourn the loss of

---

[11] Christian Maurer, *phule*," Gerhard Kittel and Gerhard Friedreich, eds., *Theological Dictionary of the New Testament*, trans. by Geoffrey W. Bromiley (Grand Rapids: Eerdmans, 1974), 9:246.

their beloved land, government, homes, friends, and Temple. We still have with us today a token of Israel's lamentation: the wailing wall in modern day Jerusalem.

Scholars remind us that

- "The temple was not only the heart of Israel's religious life but also the symbol of its national identity. . . . The patriotic as well as religious symbolism of the temple was thus enormous, and the magnificence of Herod's rebuilding matched its symbolic significance."[12]
- "The Temple was the central heart-beat of Jerusalem."[13]
- "It was the pre-eminent focus of Jewish national and religious sentiment."[14]

Indeed, after seeing the temple site shortly after its destruction, Rabbi Joshua lamented: "Woe unto us! that this, the place where the iniquities of Israel were atoned for, is laid waste!" (*Abot R. Nat.* 4).

Here again though, we may allow a less restrictive translation for argument's sake. Even if some insist on the translation "earth, world" in Matthew 24:30b, the preterist view is unharmed. Instead of locating the mourning in Israel where the scene of judgment focuses, this translation would speak of the widespread Jewish mourning throughout the world upon hearing the news. Surely the Jews throughout the world of the day would mourn Jerusalem's fall and the Temple's destruction. The other translation, though, is contextually preferable.

The clouds of heaven

The final phrase in Matthew 24:30c is:

They will see the Son of Man coming on the clouds of heaven with power and great glory.

As we consider this important phrase, we must again recall Christ's interchange with the Sanhedrin at his ecclesiastical trial which results in his crucifixion:

---

[12] R. T. France, *Mark* (Oxford: Bible Reading Fellowship, 1996), 436–37.

[13] Peter W. L. Walker, *Jesus and the Holy City: New Testament Perspectives on Jerusalem* (Grand Rapids: Eerdmans, 1996), 13.

[14] Neil Faulkner, *Apocalypse: The Great Jewish Revolt Against Rome AD 66–73* (Gloucestershire, Eng.: Tempus, 2002), 63.

> The high priest answered and said to Him, "I adjure You by the living God that You tell us if You are the Christ, the Son of God." Jesus said to him, "It is as you said. Nevertheless, I say to *you*, hereafter you will see the Son of Man sitting at the right hand of the Power, and coming on the clouds of heaven." (Matt 26:63–64)

Here Christ informs those sitting in judgment over him that they will see his coming. As I argue above, this is not a physical, visible coming, but a judgment-coming upon Jerusalem. They "see" it in the sense we "see" how a math problem works: with the "eye of understanding" rather than the organ of vision. This is like Jesus' statement regarding parables in Matthew 13:13: "Therefore I speak to them in parables; because while seeing they do not see, and while hearing they do not hear, nor do they understand" (though the word "see" in Greek is a different term).

Again we must recall that the "coming" that the Sanhedrin (Matt 26:64) and Israel at large (Matt 24:30) will witness is like Jehovah's coming against Egypt in the Old Testament: "The burden against Egypt. Behold, the Lord rides on a swift cloud, and will come into Egypt" (Isa 19:1). The Lord did not physically ride on a cloud down into Egypt. I agree with Dallas Seminary's Bible Knowledge Commentary: Isaiah 19:1 speaks of "the impending Assyrian advance" under "God's judgment."[15] Likewise, neither is it exegetically necessary that the "coming of the Son of Man" be a physical coming that the Sanhedrin will see. Because Israel rejects her Messiah (Matt 23:37; John 1:11; Acts 26:7), he judges her.

The Great Jubilee (Matt 24:31)

I move now to Matthew 24:31:

> "And He will send forth His angels with a great trumpet and they will gather together His elect from the four winds, from one end of the sky to the other."

Dispensational confusion

The surface appearance in this verse of an eschatological rapture or the second advent seems amenable to the dispensational system: "they will gather together His elect from the four winds," at the "trumpet" sound issued by "angels." Yet classic dispensationalism has such a pandemonium of theological qualifications, historical compartments, redemptive peoples, eschatological phenomena, revelational programs, law

---

[15] John A. Martin, "Isaiah," *BKC:OT*, 1065.

principles, and so forth, that this passage really expresses the system's weaknesses, rather than demonstrating its strength.

Walvoord writes of this verse:

> Some[16] have taken the elect here to refer specifically to the elect living on earth, but it is more probable that this event will include all the elect, or the saved, including Old Testament saints, saved Israel, the church,[17] and the saints of the Tribulation period leading up to the Second Coming. Some will need to be resurrected from the dead, such as the martyrs (Rev. 20:4–6) and the Old Testament saints (Dan. 12:2). The church was resurrected, or translated, earlier, at the time of the Rapture. At the second coming of Christ no child of God will be left unresurrected or unrestored, but all will share in the millennial kingdom.[18]

Notice the multiplying of peoples here. The general resurrection of amillennialism and postmillennialism divides people into two classes: the saved and the lost. But when talk of the resurrection arises, dispensationalists must account for various classes of peoples in their respective programs, resurrections, judgments, rewards, eternal destinies, and so forth.

For example, notice the following partial listing of judgments by Walvoord: "According to the Scriptures a series of judgments is related to Christ's return. . . . The martyred dead of the great Tribulation will be judged and rewarded [Rev 20:4]. In addition, Israel will be judged (Eze 20:33–38), and the Gentiles will be judged (Matt 25:31–46). These judgments precede and lead up to the millennial kingdom."[19] Thus, "while all the righteous will be raised before the Millennium, individuals will retain their identities and their group identifications such as Gentile believers and believers in Israel in the Old Testament, the church of the New Testament, and saints of the Tribulation."[20]

---

[16] One of the "some" is J. Dwight Pentecost, who teaches that this verse speaks of the "regathering of Israel." J. Dwight Pentecost, *Things to Come: A Study in Biblical Eschatology* (Grand Rapids: Zondervan, 1958), 282; J. Dwight Pentecost, *Thy Kingdom Come* (Wheaton: Victor, 1990), 255.

[17] Pentecost comments: "the reference to 'his elect' (v. 31) could not possibly refer to the church." Pentecost, *Thy Kingdom Come*, 255.

[18] John F. Walvoord, *Prophecy Knowledge Handbook* (Wheaton, Ill.: Victor, 1990), 390.

[19] John F. Walvoord, "Revelation," BKC:NT, 980.

[20] Walvoord, "Revelation," 980.

Of Matthew 24:31 Walvoord defines the elect in terms of the various dispensationally imposed categories: "Old Testament saints, saved Israel, the church, and the saints of the Tribulation period." Fortunately, the timing of this resurrection is such that it does not have to account for another group of the righteous: those who die in the millennium after conversion to Christ.[21] Walvoord explains that the "first resurrection" language of Revelation 20 actually "supports the conclusion that the resurrection of the righteous is by stages." These stages include the church at the Rapture, the two witnesses in the Tribulation, the Tribulation martyrs soon after Christ's return to earth, and the Old Testament saints.[22]

Redemptive jubilee

A more reasonable interpretation of Matthew 24:31 is to view this angelic trumpeting as a symbolical statement announcing the arrival of the ultimate Jubilee Year. With the fulfilling of the old covenant in the person and work of Christ, man's ultimate debt is forgiven: his sin debt to God. The "day of salvation" has come and now the good news will spread to the nations. Let me explain the Jubilee typology, then show how it serves as Jesus' backdrop as he teaches his Jewish (old covenant) disciples.

In the Old Testament the sabbath year was a God-ordained year of rest for the land which was to occur every seventh year:

> Speak to the sons of Israel, and say to them, "When you come into the land which I shall give you, then the land shall have a sabbath to the Lord. . . . During the seventh year the land shall have a sabbath rest, a sabbath to the Lord; you shall not sow your field nor prune your vineyard." (Lev 25:2, 4)

Built on this sabbath year of rest was the Jubilee Year. This Jubilee was the year that followed after seven consecutive sabbath years. That is, the Jubilee occurs after the passing of seven sevens, or after forty-nine years. Under this law every fiftieth year was to culminate all of the sabba-

---

[21] "In the millennial kingdom it will be a time of great joy and rejoicing and deliverance for the people of God, but death and sin will still be present." Walvoord, *Prophecy Knowledge Handbook*, 119. In fact, Walvoord seems oblivious to the fate of deceased millennial saints, for he never mentions them in his Revelation exposition in *Bible Knowledge Commentary*.

[22] Walvoord, "Revelation," *Bible Knowledge Commentary*, 980.

tical tokens of rest. In the Year of Jubilee all of Israel was to experience release from bondage and debt:

> You shall thus consecrate the fiftieth year and proclaim a release through the land to all its inhabitants. It shall be a jubilee for you, and each of you shall return to his own property, and each of you shall return to his family. You shall have the fiftieth year as a jubilee; you shall not sow, nor reap its aftergrowth, nor gather in from its untrimmed vines. For it is a jubilee; it shall be holy to you. You shall eat its crops out of the field.
>
> On this year of jubilee each of you shall return to his own property. If you make a sale, moreover, to your friend, or buy from your friend's hand, you shall not wrong one another. (Lev 25:10–14)

The typology of redemption contained in the Jubilee legislation lent it a beautiful prophetic utility. Isaiah employs Jubilee imagery to prophesy of the coming ultimate Jubilee:

> The Spirit of the Lord God is upon Me, because the Lord has anointed Me to preach good tidings to the poor; He has sent Me to heal the brokenhearted, to proclaim liberty to the captives, and the opening of the prison to those who are bound; to proclaim the acceptable year of the Lord, and the day of vengeance of our God. (Isa. 61:1–2)

Since the full redemption typified in the Jubilee comes through the work of Jesus Christ, he introduces its fulfillment in his ministry. He does this in the synagogue in Nazareth when he preaches from the Isaiah 61 passage stated above:

> And He was handed the book of the prophet Isaiah. And when He had opened the book, He found the place where it was written: "The Spirit of the LORD is upon Me, because He has anointed Me to preach the gospel to the poor. He has sent Me to heal the brokenhearted, to preach deliverance to the captives and recovery of sight to the blind, to set at liberty those who are oppressed, to preach the acceptable year of the LORD." Then He closed the book, and gave it back to the attendant and sat down. And the eyes of all who were in the synagogue were fixed on Him. And He began to say to them, "Today this Scripture is fulfilled in your hearing." (Luke 4:17–21)

Now back to Matthew 24:31. When Jesus employs imagery drawn from the Year of Jubilee legislation in Leviticus 25, he is speaking of the final stage of redemption which he brings to pass. This redemptive culmination begins in his earthly ministry, as we may surmise from such passages as Mark 1:15: "The time is fulfilled, and the kingdom of God is at hand. Repent, and believe in the gospel." Thus, Christ's ministry introduces "the acceptable year of the Lord" (Luke 4:19), "the day of salvation"

(2 Cor 6:6), which the righteous of the Old Testament longed to see (Matt 13:17).

This is why Jesus mentions the sounding of the "trumpet" in Matthew 24:31. It was the means for announcing the Jubilee, for we read in Leviticus 25:9: "You shall then sound a ram's horn abroad on the tenth day of the seventh month; on the day of atonement you shall sound a horn all through your land."[23] Thus, according to the imagery of Matthew 24:31, when the Temple order collapses Christ's "angels" will go forth into all nations joyfully trumpeting the gospel of salvific liberation: "And He will send His angels with a great sound of a trumpet, and they will gather together His elect from the four winds, from one end of heaven to the other." The strong word of God may be expressed as a "voice like a trumpet" (Isa 27:13; 58:1; Jer 6:17; Rev 1:10; 4:1).

The word for "angel" here is *aggelos* in the Greek. It can be translated "messengers," signifying human messengers, as in Matthew 11:10 and several other places in Scripture.[24] It does not seem to refer to the supernatural heavenly beings here. Rather the idea here is that those who know Christ as Savior will go forth into all the earth proclaiming the message of full salvation, the removal of man's sin debt to God.

But even if we interpret this as a reference to angels, it could then refer "to the supernatural power which lies behind such preaching."[25] Upon this interpretation it would teach that the angels of God attend the faithful proclamation of the gospel message. The Scriptures teach that God's angels are interested in and involved with his saving work among men (Luke 12:8–9; 15:10; Acts 8:26; 10:3–6, 22; 1 Pet 1:12; Rev 14:6).

The gathering of the elect

It is particularly after the fall of Jerusalem that the Church is freed from its bondage to Judaism. This occurs so that she might become a truly universal Church, rather than a racially-focused, geographically-confined people. A major problem plaguing the pre-AD 70 church is its Judaizing tendencies, as is evident in Acts 10, 11, 15, Galatians, and

---

[23] The ram's horn served as a trumpet (Josh 6:6, 8, 13; Hos 5:8). In Lev 25:9 the LXX translates "horn" with the Greek word for trumpet.

[24] Mark 1:2; Luke 7:24, 27; 9:52. See: LXX at 2 Chron 36:15–16; Hag 1:13; Mal 2:7.

[25] R. T. France, *Matthew* (TNTC) (Downers Grove, Ill.: Inter-Varsity Press, 1985), 345. This is the best commentary for studying the Olivet Discourse.

Hebrews. This is a serious threat to the universality and advance of the Christian message. As Boice notes in his commentary on Galatians, if this Judaizing tendency continues "Christianity would lose its distinctive character and soon become little more than a minor sect of Judaism."[26]

Though the mission to the Gentiles actually begins before Jerusalem's fall, Christ highlights AD 70 as the ultimate spark to the worldwide mission. Indeed, the events of AD 70 finally separate Christianity from Judaism. As Gibbs notes, this pattern of Israel-judgment then Gentile-mission appears in several of Jesus' parables.[27] To illustrate this let us consider two parables.

In Matthew 21:38–45 the Parable of the Landowner teaches that Israel's religious leaders who condemn Christ will be brought "to a wretched end" so that the owner of the vineyard can then "rent out the vineyard to other vine-growers" (Matt 21: 40–41). Jesus interprets this to Israel's religious authorities: "Therefore I say to you, the kingdom of God will be taken away from you, and be given to a nation producing the fruit of it" (21:43).

In Matthew 22:1–14 the Parable of the Marriage Feast teaches that the gospel was first offered to Israel but that she refused it (22:2–4). Then when Israel mistreats the gospel messengers "the king was enraged and sent his armies, and destroyed those murderers, and set their city on fire. Then he said to his slaves, 'The wedding is ready, but those who were invited were not worthy. Go therefore to the main highways, and as many as you find there, invite to the wedding feast'" (22:7–9).

So then, through gospel preaching by faithful messengers ("angels"), God gathers the elect into his kingdom from "the four winds, from one end of the sky to the other" (Matt 24:31b). In some English versions such as the KJV and NRSV the phrase "from one end of the sky to the other" is translated as "from one end of *heaven* [Gk.: *ouranos*] to the other." This rendering suggests that the elect are being gathered from heaven itself, so that it involves a miraculous, eschatological supernatural activity.

But this use of *ouranos* does not indicate that the action occurs in heaven above. Note two interpretive clues: (1) This language parallels the preceding phrase: "from the four winds" (i.e., the four points of the

---

[26] James M. Boice in *The Expositor's Bible Commentary*, ed. Frank E. Gaebelein (Grand Rapids: Zondervan/Regency, 1976), 10:410.

[27] Jeffrey A. Gibbs, *Jerusalem and Parousia: Jesus' Eschatological Discourse in Matthew's Gospel* (St. Louis: Concordia Academic Press, 2000), 201–04.

compass). (2) In Scripture such language often signifies simply "from horizon to horizon" (Deut 30:4; Neh 1:9; cp. Matt 8:11; Luke 13:28–29). In fact, the LXX version of Deuteronomy 30:4 reads: "from the end of heaven to the end of heaven."[28] Hence, in Matthew 24:31 the phrase "from one end of the sky to the other" means from one direction where we see the sky "touch" the horizon, to the opposite direction.

So then, here these two world-encompassing phrases speak of evangelistic success spreading throughout the earth. Consequently, this statement picks up on the theme presented in the parables of the landowner and the marriage feast in Matthew 21 and 22 and anticipates the coming "Great Commission" (Matt 28:19). These phrases hold forth the promise of the fulfillment of the Old Testament prophecies, such as Psalm 22:27: "All the ends of the earth will remember and turn to the Lord, / And all the families of the nations will worship before Thee." And Psalm 2:8: "Ask of Me, and I will surely give the nations as Thine inheritance, / And the very ends of the earth as Thy possession."[29]

The "gathering together" is the translation of the Greek *episunaxousin* which is the future tense of *episunago* (you will recognize the word "synagogue" is related to this word). This word only appears three times in Matthew. Besides this use in 24:31 it appears two times in 23:37 where Jesus laments:

> O Jerusalem, Jerusalem, who kills the prophets and stones those who are sent to her! How often I wanted to gather [*episunagagein*] your children together, the way a hen gathers [*episunagei*] her chicks under her wings, and you were unwilling.

Obviously the second usage regarding gathering chicks is intended to illustrate the first. Here Jesus longs to gather disciples to himself from Jerusalem. This gathering of disciples is the same meaning in 24:31.

The word *episunago* also appears in Hebrews 10:25 where it urges Jewish converts (hence, "The Epistle to the Hebrews") not to forsake "assembling together" *in the church*. That is, he is warning them not to leave Christianity and return to Judaism, especially in that they should "see the day drawing near," i.e., the day of Israel's judgment in AD 70. James 2:2 uses the root *sunagoge* in speaking of a church assembly: "If a man comes into your assembly [*sunagoge*]. . . ."

---

[28] The Greek reads: *ap akrou tou ouranou eos akrou tou ouranou*.

[29] See also: Psa 65:5, 8; 66:4; 67:7; 72:8; 86:9; 98:3; Isa 45:22; 66:23; Mic 5:4; Zeph 9:10.

Conclusion

We must realize the significance of the collapse of Jerusalem in AD 70. Not only does it dramatically conclude the old covenant (cp. Heb 8:13; cf. John 4:21–23; Gal 4:21–31). . . . Not only does it judge Israel for rejecting her Messiah (Matt 21:33–45; 22:1–14; 23:37–24:2) . . . . But it effectively removes a major hindrance to the spread of the Christian faith.

We see this particularly in two respects:

First, the Jewish ceremonial laws confuse many early Christians — since the earliest Christians were Jewish. Circumcision is particularly troublesome in that some deem it necessary for salvation (Acts 15:1; Gal 5:1–6; Phil 3:1–3). The growing danger exists that Christianity will be a mere sect of Judaism, as the Roman imperial government originally assumes. With the Temple's destruction, this tendency will subside as it becomes evident Christianity is now a distinct religion.

Second, the first persecutors of the faith are the Jews (Acts 8:1ff). With the AD 70 demise of the Jews' strength and the decline in their legal status with Rome, Christianity receives less resistance from them. Jewish persecution of Christians does not cease altogether (Polycarp is a dramatic case in point), but it is greatly hampered.

Chapter 8
THE TRANSITION PASSAGE
Matthew 24:32–36

I have shown that the Olivet Discourse is something of a climactic highpoint in Matthew's Gospel. Early on in his Gospel Matthew begins pointing to the coming inclusion of the Gentiles in God's plan for history. This should have been expected from the Abrahamic Covenant (Gen 12:3; 22:18; 26:4; Acts 3:25; Gal 3:8) as well as from the prophets (e.g., Psa 22:27–28; 86:9; Isa 19:19–25; 66:23; Mic 4:1–3). At the same time he begins building a case against Israel, showing her unbelief and coming judgment for not being faithful to God's calling and not receiving the Messiah (Matt 8:11–12; 23:37–38). The large Discourse covering Matthew 24 and 25 presents that judgment.

But we have only worked our way through Matthew 24:31, which covers just one-fourth of the Discourse. What about the even larger section that remains, Matthew 24:32–25:46? How shall we understand that material?

The Parable of the Fig Tree

In approaching the remainder of the Discourse we must bear in mind that the disciples originally think that Jesus' prophecy of the destruction of the temple (Matt 24:2) requires the simultaneous conclusion to history. We see this in their question that sparks the Discourse: "as He was sitting on the Mount of Olives, the disciples came to Him privately, saying, 'Tell us, *when* [Gk.: *pote*] will these things be, and *what* [Gk.: *ti*] will be the sign of Your coming, and of the end of the age?'" (24:3).

I noted in chapter three above that their question is two-fold.[1] They were asking *when* the destruction of the temple would occur. And because of their false assumption regarding its permanence they also asked:

---

[1] See France, *Matthew* (NICNT), 889–96, 936–40; Gibbs, *Jerusalem and Parousia*, 167–74.

what will be the sign of your coming to effect the end of history? We must remember that the disciples are often confused at Jesus' teaching.[2]

As we saw in chapter 3 above, a simple, straightforward reading of Matthew 24:34 presents us with an unambiguous assertion that *all* of the things Christ mentions up to this point — that is, all things in verses 4 through 34 (excluding v 27) — are to occur *in the very generation of the original disciples*: "Truly I say to you, this generation will not pass away until all these things take place." Here in Matthew 24 the phrase "this generation" speaks of the same period as "this generation" in Matthew 23:36. And in Matthew 23 the Lord is rebuking the Scribes and Pharisees *of his own day* (23:13–16, 23, 25, 27, 29). Then in verse 36 he warns them: "I say to you, all these things will come upon this generation." We may not catapult two thousand years into the future these woes upon the Pharisees. Nor should we do so with the "this generation" statement of 24:34.

Here we must remind ourselves that a series of divinely ordained signs will precede the approaching destruction of the Temple (Matt 24:4ff). The first few signs are general indicators of the final judgment on the Temple: "All these things are merely the beginning of birth pangs" (24:8). We saw that all of these signs do, in fact, come to pass in the era before AD 70. And now he informs the disciples that just as surely as fig leaves indicate approaching summer (24:32), so the events of Matthew 24:4–28 signify the approaching destruction of the temple. But verses 29–31 speak of that event actually coming and of its immediate consequence: the beginning of worldwide redemption.

The Hinge Passage

As Gibbs, France, and others argue, the Olivet Discourse has a two-part structure which corresponds to the disciples' two questions in Matthew 24:3.[3] Their first question asks "when" the destruction of the temple will occur: it is answered in vv 4–31. Their second question regards "what" will be sign of "Your coming": this is answered in 24:36–25:46.

---

[2] See: Matt 14:17, 31; 15:15, 33; 16:5–12, 22; 17:10; 18:21; 19:10, 13, 25; 20:24; Acts 11:18.

[3] Jeffrey A. Gibbs, *Jerusalem and Parousia: Jesus' Eschatological Discourse in Matthew's Gospel* (St. Louis: Concordia Academic Press, 2000), 167–81. France, *Matthew* (NICNT), 889–96

But how do we *know* this is the intended structure of the passage? It is one thing to *declare* a two-part structure while it is another to *prove* it.

Let us now look at the evidence that Jesus is shifting his attention from the destruction of the temple in AD 70 to his second coming at the end of history. I will present more than a dozen arguments for the transition in Matthew 24.

1. Argument from concluding statement

By all appearance Matthew 24:34 functions as a *concluding* statement; it seems to *end* the preceding prophecy: "Truly I say to you, this generation will not pass away until all these things take place." Why would such a statement be inserted one-fourth of the way through the discourse if it were dealing *in its entirety* with events that were to occur in "this generation"? Such would not make sense. That would be like someone giving a speech, and after fifteen minutes saying, "In conclusion," then continuing the speech for another forty-five minutes.

In addition, the Lord's very next statement helps confirm our suspicions: "Heaven and earth will pass away, but My words shall not pass away" (Matt 24:35). Here he is confirming his *previous* words. He is declaring *their* certainty: his prophetic words are more sure than even the stability of heaven and earth (cp. Matt 5:18).

Consequently, we must understand Matthew 24:34 as serving to close out one portion of the Discourse. At this point Jesus is announcing that he has answered the disciples' question regarding "when" these things shall be (Matt 24:3). He still has their next question before him. This then means that the following material relates to events *not* occurring in "*this generation*." Thus, all prophecies before verse 34 are to transpire within the disciples' own first-century generation.

2. Argument from transition indicator

In Matthew 24:36 we come upon an subject-matter transition device: "*But of* that day and hour no one knows." The introductory phrase here in the Greek is: *peri de* ("but of, concerning, regarding"). This grammatical structure suggests a transition in the passage involving a change of subject.

We may see this phrase frequently marking off new material, as in Matthew 22:31; Acts 21:25; 1 Thessalonians 4:9; and 5:1. Allow me to quickly focus on several very clear subject-transition uses of *peri de* in 1 Corinthians. There we see that Paul is turning his attention to one question after another that the Corinthians asked him: "Now concerning the things about which you wrote" (1 Cor 7:1). "Now concerning virgins" (7:25). "Now concerning things sacrificed to idols" (8:1). "Now concerning spiritual gifts, brethren" (12:1). In each case he is clearly introducing new subjects that respond to different questions presented to him.

Returning to Matthew 24, France notes that verse 36 "marks a deliberate change of subject"[4] Elsewhere he states that it is a "rhetorical formula for a new beginning."[5] Nolland agrees when he states that *peri de* functions in Matthew 24:36 as "an introductory piece for 24:37– 25:30."[6]

What is more, Gibbs demonstrates that the lone preposition *peri* in and of itself can have a resumptive force.[7] That is, *peri* ("concerning") can pick up on a subject broached earlier in a narrative by serving as a sign that the speaker is returning to that issue once again. Gibbs offers two illustrations from Matthew's Gospel.

In Matthew 6:25 Jesus challenges his followers not to be anxious regarding *for both* "what you shall eat" (food) *and* "what you shall put on" (clothing). Then in verse 26 he immediately urges them to "look at the birds" to observe that "your heavenly Father feeds them." He intends this to resolve their first anxiety regarding food. Then in v 28 he returns to his original exhortation in v 25 and picks up on their second concern, *clothing*: "And why [*kai peri*] are you anxious about clothing?" (6:28). Thus, his instruction in verses 28 and 29 picks up on a portion of his earlier statement in v 25; it *resumes* his initial concern regarding clothing.

The same function operates in Matthew 22. In vv 23–28 the Sadducees "came to Him and questioned Him" about the resurrection, giving a hypothetical example of a man who was married seven times. In vv 29–30 Jesus deals with their example, then in v 31 he reaches back to their original question about the resurrection and states: "but regarding [*peri de*] the resurrection of the dead, have you not read. . . ?" Once again we see the resumptive force of the preposition *peri*.

So now for our purposes: in Matthew 24:36 *peri* reaches back to the disciples' *second* question of the two that were raised in v 3. Having dealt with their *first* question in vv 4–35, he now returns to consider their

---

[4] R. T. France, *Matthew* (TNTC) (Downers Grove, Ill.: InterVarsity, 1985), 347.

[5] France, *Matthew* (NICNT), 936.

[6] John Nolland, *The Gospel of Matthew* (NIGTC) (Grand Rapids: Eerdmans, 2005), 990.

[7] Gibbs, *Jerusalem and Parousia*, 172.

second one. By this structuring of the passage we see that v 36 introduces new material differing from vv 4–35. At this point he moves away from his AD 70 prophecy and begins speaking of his second advent at the "end of the age," which he will cover in 24:36–25:46.

3. Argument from humiliation limitation

Focusing once again on Matthew 24:36 we read: "But of that day and hour no one knows, not even the angels of heaven, *nor the Son*, but the Father alone." Here Christ states that in his state of humiliation (the period from the time of his earthly conception within Mary's womb until his glorification at his resurrection) he himself has no knowledge as to when "that day and hour" will occur. But of what "day and hour" is he speaking?

He must be speaking of his future second advent because in the preceding section of his Discourse he tells his disciples that numerous signs will be given, but that "the end [of the temple] is not yet" (Matt 24:6). This indicates that he definitely knows when *that* event will occur. He also dogmatically teaches them that these earlier things will certainly happen in "this generation" (24:34). Thus, as Nolland notes: "there is a deliberate contrast between the confident tone of the predictive materials thus far in the chapter, climaxing in v. 34, and the present insistence that only the Father knows."[8]

4. Argument from temporal markers

As we continue looking at Matthew 24:36 we also note that it lacks any temporal-transition markers to link it with the preceding events. It is wholly unconnected with the preceding material in terms of temporal progression. This is surprising in that in the preceding material we see a well-connected historical progress with recurring "then" statements (24:9, 14, 16, 21, 23, 30), as well as an "immediately after" (24:29) declaration.

But when Christ makes the statement in Matthew 24:36 we hear nothing that links it with the preceding material. We hear absolutely no "then" or "after" nor any other such temporal progress indicator. Thus, as France notes: "its contents stand apart from the historical sequence hitherto described."[9] This is because it is distantly separated from the

---

[8] Nolland, *Matthew*, 991.
[9] France, *Matthew* (NICNT), 983.

events of AD 70 (see numbers 5 and 13 below where he contrasts near events with distant ones).

5. Argument from demonstrative distinction

In Matthew 24:34–36 provides further evidence of a subject transition. Jesus contrasts near and far events:

> Truly I say to you, *this* generation will not pass away until all *these* things take place (Matt 24:34).
> But of *that* day and hour no one knows, not even the angels of heaven, nor the Son, but the Father alone. (24:36)

In this passage "*this* generation" is set in contrast to "*that* day." With these words the Lord looks beyond the signs just given for "this generation" (*haute*, near demonstrative, 24:34) to the event of "that day" (*ekeines*, far demonstrative) (24:36). Thus, the Lord's attention turns to his distant second advent at the end of history.

6. Argument from observational prospects

Before his statement in Matthew 24:34 Christ mentions numerous events that serve as historical signs, events such as: "wars and rumors of wars" (Matt 24:6), "famines and earthquakes" (v 7), "false prophets" (v 11), and so forth. He specifically mentions a pre-eminent sign: "the sign of the Son of Man."

Furthermore, he personalizes this portion of his Discourse by repeatedly warning the very disciples sitting before him on the Mount of Olives (Matt 24:3):

> "see to it that no one misleads *you*" (Matt 24:4)
> "*you* will be hearing of wars" (v 6a)
> "see that *you* are not frightened" (v 6b)
> "they will deliver *you* to tribulation, and will kill *you*" (v 9)
> "when *you* see the Abomination of Desolation" (v 15)
> "if anyone says to *you*" (v 23)
> "behold, I have told *you* in advance" (v 25)
> "if therefore they say to *you*" (v 26)
> "*you* too, when *you* see all these things" (v 33)

Thus, he is informing his disciples (who asked him the questions) how *they* might know the time of the coming end of the temple; it is a predictable event.

In fact, the Lord even gives the disciples a parable illustrating how the event coming in their lifetimes can be known, urging them to properly read all the signs:

> Now learn the parable from the fig tree: when its branch has already become tender, and puts forth its leaves, you know that summer is near; even so you too, when you see all these things, recognize that He is near, right at the door. (Matt 24:32–33)

But after Matthew 24:34 Jesus drops all mention of signs and predictability. Instead he includes statements emphasizing absolute surprise and total unpredictability:

> "But of that day and hour no one knows, not even the angels of heaven, nor the Son, but the Father alone" (24:36)
> "they did not understand" (v 39)
> "you do not know" (v 42)
> "if the head of the house had known" (v 43)
> "coming at an hour when you do not think He will" (v 44)
> "he does not expect him" (v 50)
> "you do not know" (25:13)

This indicates that the following section involves an event that is coming at an altogether unknown and indeterminable time. He is no longer speaking of the destruction of the temple in AD 70, but his second coming in the distant future.

7. Argument from multiple days

By the very nature of the case, the numerous events leading up to the Roman military destruction of the temple in AD 70 will require a number of days. Hence, in the portion of his Discourse prior to Matthew 24:36 Jesus mentions "those *days* [plural]" (v 19, 29) and even comforts his disciples by noting that "those *days*" will be "cut short" (v 22).

This mention of the *days* of the tribulation period are set in stark contrast to the singular *day* — indeed, the exact moment — of the second coming: "But of that *day* and *hour* no one knows, not even the angels of heaven, nor the Son, but the Father alone" (Matt 24:36). After this transition at 24:36 he repeatedly mentions the singular "day" (24:42, 50) or "the day" and "the hour" (25:13). The second advent does not involve a series of historical actions, as is the case with the Roman military operations against the Jews, Jerusalem, and the temple. The second advent is a one-time, catastrophic event conducted by a singular individual, Christ himself.

8. Argument from deception fears

In the first part of the Discourse Jesus repeatedly warns of the danger of deception by those who would "mislead" (*planaō*) :

> "And Jesus answered and said to them, 'See to it that no one misleads you. For many will come in My name, saying, "I am the Christ," and will mislead many.'" (Matt 24:4–5)
> "And many false prophets will arise, and will mislead many." (24:11)
> "For false Christs and false prophets will arise and will show great signs and wonders, so as to mislead, if possible, even the elect." (24:24)

Furthermore, we should note that he even mentions deception caused by false Christs (Matt 24:5, 23–27) and false prophets (24:11, 24). The false Christs will deceive many by claiming to be Christ himself (24:5), while many people will claim that Christ is here or there (24:23).

Indeed, the Lord warns that these are obvious deceivers because when he returns in his second advent it will be impossible to miss, no deception will be possible: "For just as the lightning comes from the east, and flashes even to the west, so shall the coming of the Son of Man be" (Matt 24:27).

All of this serves as a significant indicator of a subject shift when we compare this to his teaching after Matthew 24:36. After that point he no longer mentions the danger of deceit: the word *planaō* ("mislead") vanishes from the narrative. In fact, the second advent will suddenly overwhelm people in the midst of their daily activities: they will be eating, and drinking and marrying (Matt 24:38–39). They will be working in the field (v 40). They will be grinding at the mill (v 41). They will be as surprised as one whose house is broken into without warning (v 43).

Contrary to this, no one would be surprised at the destruction of the temple in AD 70. After all, the Romans took five months of relentless siege warfare to get into Jerusalem and destroy the temple after they encircled Jerusalem in April, AD 70. And even this occurs well after the formal engagement of the Jewish War in the Spring of AD 67 and the early military operations in Galilee and elsewhere.

9. Argument from social contrasts

The social circumstances of the early portion of the Olivet Discourse dramatically differ from those of the latter portion. In the first section (up to Matt 24:36) all is chaotic, dangerous, and confused. This period is laden with wars and rumors of wars (Matt 24:6–7), famines and earthquakes (v 7), betrayal and persecution (v 10), lawlessness (v 12), and great tribulation (v 21). Thus, woe upon woe befalls men in the chaotic first portion of the Discourse.

But in the second section all of this upheaval and danger disappears. Social activities appear tranquil, allowing business as usual while the mundane activities of life continue. People are marrying and eating and drinking (Matt 24:38), working in the field (v 40), and grinding at the mill (v 41). The wholesale chaos leading up to AD 70 stands in stark contrast to the peaceable conditions at the time of Christ's second coming.

10. Argument from flight opportunity

In the first section Christ urges desperate flight from the area, clearly implying there will be time and opportunity to flee: "then let those who are in Judea flee to the mountains" (Matt 24:16). In fact, one particular sign — the abomination of desolation — will be the cue to leave the area. Because of this opportunity of flight, many lives of God's elect will be saved: "unless those days had been cut short, no life would have been saved; but for the sake of the elect those days shall be cut short" (24:22).

But upon entering the second section of the Discourse we hear of no commands to escape, no opportunities for flight. Indeed, we witness just the opposite. Once again we can read through the warnings of the unpredictable nature of the second advent (as in # 6 above) and realize that by the very nature of the case no opportunity for flight will exist:

> "But of that day and hour no one knows, not even the angels of heaven, nor the Son, but the Father alone" (24:36)
> "they did not understand" (v 39)
> "you do not know" (v 42)
> "if the head of the house had known" (v 43)
> "coming at an hour when you do not think He will" (v 44)
> "he does not expect him" (v 50)
> "you do not know" (25:13)

11. Argument from narrative function

Gibbs notes that when we compare the two sections of the Lord's Olivet Discourse we may quickly note that the first section issues *warnings* regarding deception and danger.[10] For instance, we hear: "see to it that no one misleads you" (Matt 24:4); "you will be hearing of wars"

---

[10] Gibbs, *Jerusalem and Parousia*, 172.

(24:6); "they will deliver you to tribulation, and will kill you" (24:9); and so forth.

The second section of the narrative differs in tone by issuing *exhortations* related to future judgment and reward, calling upon the reader to exercise faithfulness and diligence. The reader is exhorted to "be on the alert" (Matt 24:42); to "be ready" (24:44), with the result that he will be considered "the faithful and sensible slave" (24:45). Jesus also gives a parable contrasting the foolish and the prudent (25:1–12) which ends with an exhortation to "be on the alert then" (25:13). In addition he presents a parable on the trustworthy and the untrustworthy slaves (25:14–30). The slaves who invest for the future are each commended as being "a good and faithful slave" (25:21, 23).

Then in Matthew 25:31–46 the Lord speaks of the final judgment "when the Son of Man comes in His glory, and all the angels with Him" (Matt 25:31a). Here he "separates the sheep from the goats" (25:32b) based on the evidence of their true conversion exhibited by their love for Christ and his people (25:35–46). Thus, he so frames the final judgment that it serves as an exhortation to continuance in the faith and among God's people.

Fearful warnings of imminent danger in the earlier section greatly differ from moral exhortations to long-term faithfulness and preparedness in the latter section. This difference demonstrates what we have seen on the basis of other considerations, that is, that these two sections are fundamentally different.

12. Argument from eschatological contrast

Jesus appears to use key terms that distinguish his metaphorical coming in AD 70 from his literal coming at the second advent. In Matthew 24:4–34 ne never uses the word *parousia* ("coming," "presence") — except in v 27 where he intentionally distinguishes his visible second advent from the first-century (24:34) deceptions which claim Jesus is hidden here or there (24:24–26).

This is significant in that the disciples' original question regarding his "coming" uses the word *parousia*: "what will be the sign of Your coming [*parousia*]" (Matt 24:3). Yet Jesus studiously avoids the term to describe events occurring in the first section, though he does use the word *erchomenos* ("coming") in the key verse at 24:30: "then the sign of the Son of Man will appear in the sky, and then all the tribes of the earth will mourn, and they will see the Son of Man coming [*erchomenos*] on the clouds of the sky with power and great glory."

After Matthew 24:34, though, he twice uses *parousia* of that unpredictable coming in the distant future:

"For the coming [*parousia*] of the Son of Man will be just like the days of Noah." (24:37)

"They did not understand until the flood came and took them all away; so shall the coming [*parousia*] of the Son of Man be." (v 39)

13. Argument from temporal duration

In the early section of Matthew 24 the time frame is short. The disciples will be facing real dangers that will transpire in "this generation" (Matt 24:34). They are to be on the lookout for various signs, especially that one that occurs within the then-standing temple (24:15), for then they are to flee the area (24:16). This all fits with Jesus' introductory warning of the judgment that will befall the scribes and Pharisees — also in "this generation" (23:34–36).

In the following section from Matthew 24:36 and into chapter 25 the time frame is much longer. No more do we hear of "this generation," rather Jesus' parables anticipate a distant future:

"But if that evil servant says in his heart, 'My master is *delaying* his coming.'" (Matt 24:48)

"But while the bridegroom was *delayed*, they all slumbered and slept." (Matt 25:5)

"After a *long time* the lord of those servants came and settled accounts with them." (Matt 25:19)

Conclusion

Although the Olivet Discourse is a favorite of date-setting populists, it should not be so. The verses of Matthew 24:4–34, so often set in *our* approaching future, actually occur in our distant past. Indeed, Christ specifically denies the possibility of dating his second coming (Matt 24:36ff) despite dispensational tendencies to date-setting.

Many contemporary Christians believe beyond any doubt that we are living in the very last days before Christ's return. Yet our parents and grandparents living through World Wars I and II seemingly had what they could consider even clearer "signs." Hear the words of an earlier prophetic writer. Writing in 1918 Arthur W. Pink sounds the alarm:

> Brethren, the end of the Age is upon us. All over the world, reflecting minds are discerning the fact that we are on the eve of another of those far-reaching crises which make the history of our race.... Those who look out on present conditions are forced to conclude that the consummation of this dispensation is at hand. . . . The sands in the hour glass of this Day of Salvation have almost run out. The signs of the Times demonstrate it. 'But,' it may be asked, 'Have not other ages, as well as the present been crowded with signs of distress?' Undoubtedly.... They unduly magnified the evil, and erred in their calculations. . . . But today, the Signs are so plain they cannot be mis-read, though the foolish may close their eyes and refuse to examine them. What these Signs are we have shown at length in chapter six and if the evidence there furnished has not convinced the reader that the Lord is at hand, then there is little hope that any further arguments drawn from Scripture will do so.[11]

Pink was wrong then; his contemporary sympathizers are wrong today. And for the same reasons: they are mis-reading the text. Pink eventually realized his error and changed his views. I am hopeful that many more Christians will exercise such wisdom.

---

[11] A. W. Pink, *The Redeemer's Return* (Ashland, Ky.: Calvary Baptist Bookstore, rep. n.d. [1918]), 318-319.

Chapter 9
CONCLUSION

We have come a long way in our study of the Olivet Discourse (Matt 24–25). It will serve us well to rehearse what we have learned. One of the more important aspects of our study together is our avoiding the common tendency simply to jump into the exciting portions of the Lord's famous Discourse. Instead, I have carefully set this prophecy within its proper historical and literary context. This context-establishing effort took two entire chapters (chs. 1–2) but was essential for providing a secure footing for entering into the Discourse as it was intended.

In chapter 1 I surveyed the narrative flow of Matthew's whole Gospel which documents Israel's spiritual blindness and demonstrates her covenantal rebellion. As we began our walk together through Matthew, we noted from its beginning that we could see clouds gradually arising on Israel's horizon and could hear the faint rumble of distant thunder. For instance, upon hearing of the birth of Jesus the Messiah, "all Jerusalem" was troubled (Matt 2:3) — though Gentiles from the east rejoiced and worshiped him (2:10–11). And when John the Baptist appears on the scene he warns Israel of her need for repentance (3:1–2). He even rejects her religious leaders when they seek his baptism (3:7). Shortly thereafter Jesus begins preaching in Galilee of the Gentiles, fulfilling a prophecy that speaks of the Gentiles receiving light (4:12–17). Why was Jerusalem troubled? Why are the Gentiles receiving light?

As we made our way further into Matthew's story, the scattered clouds began gathering and darkening. For instance, we heard Jesus declare:

> Truly I say to you, I have not found such great faith with anyone in Israel. And I say to you, that many shall come from east and west, and recline at the table with Abraham, and Isaac, and Jacob, in the kingdom of heaven; but the sons of the kingdom shall be cast out into the outer darkness. (Matt 8:10–12)

In fact, we heard him compare Israel negatively to pagan cities in the Old Testament, including even wicked Sodom (11:20–24; 12:41–42). He even calls his generation "evil and adulterous" (Mt 12:39; 16:4). Things do not look good for Israel.

Then finally as we entered Matthew's closing chapters we saw Jesus going into Jerusalem (Matt 21–28). In that context we arrived at Jesus' climactic prophecy where we could see the destructive storm in its full fury in the Olivet Discourse.[12] Anyone reading Matthew carefully should not be surprised at Jesus' pronouncement of Israel's judgment. This does not suddenly crash unexpectedly upon the scene. Rather our author carefully prepares us for this inevitable conclusion all along the way. In our quick overview we saw that one important theme in Matthew is his presentation of the decline and fall of Israel as she rejects her Messiah.

In chapter 2 we focused on the immediate historical and literary contexts of Olivet in Matthew 23. There we saw Christ's warning to the Jewish people (Matt 23:1–12) and his rebuke of their religious authorities (23:13–36). Israel has been poorly served by her spiritual leaders. Jesus is heartbroken as he cries:

> O Jerusalem, Jerusalem, who kills the prophets and stones those who are sent to her! How often I wanted to gather your children together, the way a hen gathers her chicks under her wings, and you were unwilling. Behold, your house is being left to you desolate! For I say to you, from now on you shall not see Me until you say, "Blessed is He who comes in the name of the Lord!" (Matt 23:37–39)

Then in chapter 3 I began concentrating on the issues even more directly relevant to the Olivet Discourse. I noted that Jesus' statement regarding the temple being left "desolate" leads us directly into the Discourse itself. The Lord's lament over Jerusalem and her desolate house prompted the disciples to point out to him the majesty of the temple (Matt 24:1). Their display of wonder resulted in Jesus' response that their remarkable temple would be so devastated that "not one stone here shall be left upon another" (24:2). Upon hearing this the perplexed disciples ask: "Tell us, when will these things be, and what will be the sign of Your coming, and of the end of the age?" (24:3). Jesus answers them by giving them the Olivet Discourse.

In chapter 4 I pointed out Jesus' answer to "when" these things will be. We saw that he expressly states: "Truly I say to you, this generation will not pass away until all these things take place" (Matt 24:34). Not only

---

[12] All of my storm metaphors are in keeping with the Discourse itself. Jesus speaks of the difficulty of winter (Matt 24:20), the presence of lightning (24:27), the darkening of the sun (24:29), the gathering of clouds (24:30), and the flood (24: 38–39).

so but we saw that the Lord warns only those in Judea (the region surrounding Jerusalem) to flee (24:16). These two indicators lock us into both a first-century fulfillment and Judean-focus of the "great tribulation" (24:21).

In chapters 5—7 I provided a verse-by-verse exposition of the actual portion of the Discourse that relates to AD 70 and the temple's destruction: Matthew 24:4–31. This is the focal portion of the prophecy which is the subject of great interest and intense debate. There we saw that each of the elements in our Lord's prophecy fits perfectly within the first-century limitations which he himself puts on it. We have no compelling need to project the prophecies into our own distant future — and every reason *not* to do so.

Finally, in chapter 8 I showed over a dozen exegetical arguments that prove that Jesus spoke of both the AD 70 event as well as his second advent. The disciples thought the temple's destruction signaled the end of history. Jesus corrects them by injecting a clear transition in his prophecy distinguishing the events to transpire in his own generation to those regarding a far-distant day when he will return again. I did not give an exposition of the latter portion of the Discourse (Matt 24:36–25:46) because of the almost universal evangelical agreement that it speaks of the second advent.

It is my hope that our study of the Olivet Discourse might accomplish several important ends:

First, our study should explain this fascinating prophecy which has so captured the minds of evangelicals today. The prophecy is not only given by our Lord himself, but is his longest recorded message and the climax of his teaching ministry in Matthew which should show its significance for him.

Second, our study should provide insights into a proper contextual method for interpreting Scripture. Christians today lean too heavily on out-of-context prooftexting. Clearly a text without a context is a pretext. Clear biblical understanding results only from careful contextual analysis.

Third, it should discourage a naive commitment to some of the popular, but outlandish, expositions that dominate the Christian market today. Christians have embarrassed themselves for too long with calls for the end. Most of the verses they use for this purpose can be understood as referring to the destruction of the temple in AD 70.

When all is said and done, I believe Christ meant it when he told his disciples: "Truly I say to you, this generation will not pass away until all these things take place" (Matt 24:34). And it certainly was no accident of history that the temple was destroyed forty years later.

SELECT SCRIPTURE INDEX

Genesis
12:3 128
15:16 33
22:18 128
19:28 113

Exodus
11:6 99

Leviticus
7:18 89
20:22–26 21
25:1ff 121
25:2, 4 120
25:9 121
25:10–14 121
25:23 21

Numbers
14:11–12 80
18:21, 24, 28 44

Deuteronomy
7:25 89
13:1–4 80
27:15 89
28:15, 49–50 26
28:26 104
28:49 105
30:4 124

Joshua
18:20 113
20:40 113

Judges
4:24–5:1 109
5:4–5 109

20:38 113

2 Kings
18:5 99
23:25 99

1 Chronicles
29:3 92

2 Chronicles
36:15–16 33
36:19 33

Nehemiah
1:9 124
9:26 21, 32

Psalms
2:8 124
37:20 1113
79:3 104
103:5 105
139: 13–16 *104*

Ecclesiastes
3:11 100
10:5 104

Isaiah
5:7 21
5:8–23 26
9:1 9
13:1 109
13:6, 9 47
13:8 76
13:10, 13 109
13:17, 19 109
19:1 118

19:19–25 128
34:3–5 110
40:4 20
40:31 105
56:7 101
61:1–2 121

Jeremiah
4:11, 23–24 110
6:24 76
7:1 19
7:4 19, 33, 42
7:14–15 33
7:25–26 33
12:7 35
14:6 104
22:23 76

Lamentations
4:19 105

Ezekiel
5:9 99
11:23 39
13:5 47
20:33–38 119
32:2, 7–8 110
37:1ff 103

Daniel
8:23 33
9:1ff 66
9:24 33
9:26 91
12:2 119

Hosea
8:1 105

Joel
1:15 47
2:1, 10 110
2:1, 11 47

Amos
5:18 47

Obadiah
1:15 47

Micah
4:1–3 128
4:9–10 76
5:3 101
7:1–2 19

Zephaniah
1:7 47

Zechariah
2:12 91
9:9 17
12:10–14 116
14:4 39

Malachi
4:5 47

Matthew
1:1 6
1:17 5-6
2:3 139
2:6 115
2:13–23 7
3:7 33
3:8 8
3:9 5
3:9–12 8
3:12 8
4:5 89
4:12 9
4:12–17 139
4:15–16 9
4:17 10, 32
5:10–12 10
5:29–30 80
5:47 11

6:25	130	*18:17*	7
7:13–14	11	*19:8*	15
7:28–29	11	*19:28*	77, 115
8:10–12	8, 139	*20:17–19*	17
9:16–17	11	*21:5*	17
10:5	12, 21, 83	*21:9*	17, 66
10:16–17	24	*21:12ff*	17, 18, 37
10:16–18	16	*21:13*	18, 35
10:16–23	33	*21:15–16*	19
10:17–21	78	*21:19*	8
10:18	83	*21:9–21*	19
10:22	51, 80	*21:12*	43
10:23	12, 17, 61	*21:13*	32
10:25	83	*21:18–22*	44
10:34	22	*21:19-20*	103
10:34–36	12	*21:21*	20
11:13	19	*21:23*	44
11:14	12	*21:23–26*	19, 44
11:16	60	*21:28–32*	20, 44
11:16–19	12–13	*21:23*	21, 43
11:20	60	*21:33–45*	20
11:20–24	13, 139	*21:38–45*	123
12:39	13, 139	*21:40–41*	123
12:41–42	60	*21:42*	103
12:42	13, 60	*21:43*	8, 20, 43, 123
13:13	118	*21:43–45*	21
13:17	15, 122	*21:44*	103
13:21	80	*21:45*	21
13:39–40	48	*22:1–14*	21, 44, 123
13:49	48	*22:7*	22, 44, 104, 112
13:58	14	*22:7–9*	123
15:7–14	14	*22:15–22*	44
15:14	29	*22:23–28*	130
15:24	21, 24, 83	*22:39–40*	80
16:1	114	*22:46*	44
16:4	14	*23:1*	30
16:16	32	*23:2*	36, 44
16:18	7, 21	*23:2–3*	30–31
16:21	17, 111	*23:4*	30
16:28	14, 61	*23:5*	30
17:10–13	15	*23:1–12*	140
17:11	77	*23:12*	30, 31
17:17	15	*23:13*	31, 32

23:15 32
23:16–17 32
23:23 32
23:24 32
23:27 32
23:31 32
23:32 33, 36, 59
23:32–36 22
23:33 33
23:34–35 33
23:35 36, 59, 104
23:36 22, 33, 58, 59, 60, 61
23:36–24:3 95
23:37 27, 36, 61, 104, 124
23:37–39 33, 140
23:38 35, 36, 39, 57
23:38–24:3 89, 112
23:39 35, 39
24:1 35, 39, 40, 49, 89
24:1–3 39
24:2 19, 35, 41–42, 57, 61, 64, 65, 89, 140
24:2–3 70, 71
24:3 1, 43, 44, 46, 47, 48, 49, 65, 108, 111, 132, 136
24:4 65, 136
24:4–5 133
24:5 49, 66–70
24:6 47, 49, 56, 87, 108
24:6–7 70–73
24:7 74–76
24:8 49, 76–78, 128
24:9 136
24:10 80
24:11 134
24:11–13 78–9
24:12 80
24:13 47, 49, 80
24:14 49, 81–85, 87
24:15 35, 36, 81–85, 88–89, 90, 92, 115, 116, 137
24:15–16 57

24:15–19 57
24:15–28 ch 6
24:16 36, 57, 135
24:16–18 93
24:16–20 95
24:21–22 94, 95–96
24:22 108
24:23–28 100–05
24:26 102
24:27 102, 134
24:28 102
24:29 107–10, 131
24:29–31 ch 7
24:30 36, 109, 111, 112, 114, 115–18, 136
24:31 85, 118–24
24:32 128
24:32–33 133
24:32–36 ch 8
24:34 22, 23, ch 4, 89, 95, 107, 128, 129, 133, 137, 141
24:34–36 132
24:35 129
24:36 56, 112, 129, 130, 131, 133, 135
24:36 129–30
24:38 135
24:38–39 98
24:40 135
24:42 136
24:48 108, 137
25:1–12 136
25:5 108, 137
25:13 133
25:19 137
26:3–5 22
26:31 66
26:61 42
26:64 23, 36, 43, 114
26:47 22
26:57 22
26:58 48

26:61 22	**John**
26:63–64 118	*2:14–15* 17
26:64 116	*2:18–22* 114
26:65 23, 110	*3:13* 114
27:1 23	*419* 122
27:20 23, 111	*4:20, 23* xiii
27:22 23	*4:21* 77, 125
27:23 18	*4:21–23* 114
27:24 24	*6:15* 47
27:25 24, 25	*6:32–42* 114
27:40 42	*6:39–44* 78
27:45 115	*6:42* 114
27:51 23	*8:39* 5
27:53 89	*11:24* 78
27:62–66 111	*11:48* 31, 43
28:11–15 24, 111	*13:34–-35* 80
28:19 10, 24, 124	*15:26* 47
28:20 48	*16:13* 47
	16:21 76
Mark	*18:36–37* 47
1:15 122	*18:37* 66
3:26 48	
9:1 14, 77	**Acts**
11:13 19	*1:6* 47
11:23 20	*1:7* 47
13:1 40	*2:1ff* 47
13:2 40	*2:5* 83
13:19 98	*2:9* 112
16:19 114	*2:14* 113
	2:17 78
Luke	*2:22* 113
1:73 5	*2:23* 113
2:1 82	*2:29–31* xii
4:17–21 121	*2:33* 113
13:6–9 19	*2:34–35* 113
13:7 9	*2:36* 113
21:20 90	*2:38* 113
21:20–21 91	*2:40* 113
21:20–24 45, 56, 57	*3:19* 77
21:21 90, 91	*3:21* 77
24:25 47	*7:52–53* 33
	7:54–60 33
	8:1 61

8:9–10 68
9:1–4 61
11:28 82
13 78

Romans
1:8 84
10:17 84
10:18 84
11:11–12 35
11:25–26 35
13:8 80

1 Corinthians
7:1 130
8:1 130
10:11 78
12:1 130

2 Corinthians
3:13 48
5:17 77
6:6 121

Galatians
3:8 128
4:21–31 125
4:23–31 77
6:15 77

Ephesians
2:10 77
2:14 93
2:20–21 77
6:17 77

Philippians
3:1–3 125
3:5 116

Colossians
1:6 84
1:23 84

1 Thessalonians
2:14–16 22, 25
4:9 80

2 Thessalonians
3:1 78

2 Timothy
4:10 79
4:16 78

Hebrews
1:2 78
2:1–4 78
6:1–6 78
7:3 48
8:13 xiii, 114
9:10 77
9:26 78
10:26–31 78
12:18–28 77
12:22 77
12:27–28 77, 114

James
2:2 124
5:11 48

1 Peter
1:20 78
2:5 77

2 Peter
3:10 47

1 John
2:18 69, 78
2:19 78

Revelation
19:21 104
20:4–6 119
21:1 77

21:1–2 77
21:2–3 115
22:6, 10   77

SUBJECT AND NAME INDEX

ABOMINATION of desolation, 1, 35, 36, 57, 63, 88–90, 92, 94, 132
Abraham, 5, 6, 8, 11, 96, 139
adulterous generation, 13, 14, 139
angel(s), 33, 48, 118, 120, 122, 133, 135, 136
antichrist(s), 69
anti-Semitism, 7–8, 24, 26
apostasy, 49, 78–80

BABYLON (-ians), 6, 33, 99, 109, 113
Barabbas, 18, 23, 66
birth pangs, 49, 56, 76–77, 108, 128

CALVIN, John, 15
cloud(s), 23, 29, 36, 43, 65, 75, 109, 110,111, 113, 114, 115, 137, 139
cloud-judgment, 23
curse(s), 8, 19, 26, 74, 103, 105

DANIEL (prophet), 35, 54, 57, 66, 88, 90, 91
David, King, xii, 4, 6, 17, 66, 101
demon(s), 13, 14, 93
Dio Cassius, 75,

EAGLE(s), 26,102–05
earthquake(s), 1, 73–75, 109, 116, 132, 134
Egypt, 7, 33, 68, 99, 101, 110, 118
Elijah, 12, 15
end, the, 30, 39, 43, 47–48, 58, 60, 65, 70, 73, 81, 85, chs 6–7, 127–130

Epictetus, 71
Eusebius, 63, 71, 75, 85, 96

FALSE Christs, 1, 66–67, 100-01, 134
false prophet(s), 1, 67, 69, 79–80, 100-01, 132
famine(s), 1, 63, 73–74, 82, 132
fig tree, 9, 19–20, 28, 44, 103, 110, 127–29
flood (Noah's), 98, 137

GALLUS, Cestius, 62
gospel (genre), 4
Great Commission, 24, 81, 83, 124
great tribulation, xi, 1, 54, 56, 72, 92, 94–101, 119, 135

Henry, Matthew, 15, 16
Hippolytus, 69
holy place, 35, 57, 88, 91–92, 115

JERUSALEM, 7, 12, 14, 16, 17, 22, 33, 37, 44, 57, 62, 73, 76, 87, 92, 94, 95, 98, 99, 110, 112, 114
Jewish War, 22, 60, 62, 69, 71, 72, 76, 79, 93, 96, 100, 134
John the Baptist, 12, 15, 28
Jubilee, 118–21
Judaism, 5, 6, 11, 12, 25, 32, 122, 125
judgment-coming, 61, 102n, 118

KINGDOM of heaven/God, 8, 15, 20, 21, 26, 31, 43, 77, 121, 139

LAND of Israel, 2, 12, 115, 116

LaHaye, Tim, 1, 45
Left Behind, 1
Lighfoot, John, 16
Lindsey, Hal, xi, 1

MAGUS, Simon, 68, 69
Matthew, Gospel of, 3–4,
marriage feast, 44, 123, 124
millennium, 67, 69, 115, 119, 120
moneychangers, 17, 18, 44
Mount of Olives, 1, 20, 29, 39, 49, 55, 68, 101, 127, 132

NERO, 62, 71, 73, 78, 79
new covenant, 11, 15, 16, 77, 78, 114
new creation, 16, 77
New Israel, 5, 16
New Jerusalem, 77, 114, 115n
Nineveh, 13, 60

ORIGEN, 71

PAX Romana, 70, 71
persecute (-tion), 10, 12, 16, 22, 33, 49, 50, 59, 60, 61, 67, 69, 78, 80, 125, 134
Philo, 41, 42
Pilate, 18, 23, 24, 66
Promised Land, 7, 114, 115

RABBI(s), 14, 40, 66, 76, 97, 101, 117
race, Jewish, 53–54
rapture, 11, 12, 45, 54, 118, 120
ritual(s), 44
Rome (-ans), 22, 31, 43, 62, 72, 74, 93, 94, 97, 101, 104
    army, 42, 104

SADDUCEES, 20, 34, 44, 130
Sanhedrin, 22, 23, 31, 42, 43, 113, 116, 117, 118

scribes, 11, 17, 20, 22, 25, 28, 31, 42, 53, 59, 60, 64, 81, 109, 110, 128, 137
second advent, 45, 46, 47, 52, 102, 108, 11, 112, 118, 131, 133, 141
symbolism, 18, 19, 20, 28, 47, 103, 105, 107, 117, 120
synagogue(s), 12, 34, 53, 121, 124

TACITUS, 40, 72, 75, 78, 79
temple, 11, 17
    destruction, xii, 5, 11, 14, 22, 28, 31, 37, 57, 60, 77, 89, 98, 103, 107, 111
    glory of, 39–40, 46, 89
    permanence, 42, 47
tribes (of Israe), 15, 36, 111, 115-17, 136

UNITED Nations, 88
United States, 88
Universe, 52, 72, 84, 107

VESPASIAN, 62, 70, 90, 96

WAR(s), 1, 49–50, 70–73, 132, 134, 135
wineskins, 11

YEAR of Four Emperors, 72

ZIONISM (-ist), 47, 66,

Notes

Notes

www.ingramcontent.com/pod-product-compliance
Lightning Source LLC
Chambersburg PA
CBHW070443090426
42735CB00012B/2446